RADICAL AUTHENTICITY:

Strong Medicine For Turbulent Times

David Steele

RADICAL AUTHENTICITY: *Strong Medicine For Turbulent Times*

To learn more about David Steele's work, please contact him through his website: www.livelovenow.life.

Library of Congress Cataloging-in-Publication Data
(Steele, David).

RADICAL AUTHENTICITY: *Strong Medicine For Turbulent Times*

ISBN: # 9781513656700 (Paperback)
ISBN: # 9781513656717 (eBook)

OCC019000 BODY, MIND & SPIRIT / Inspiration & Personal Growth
SEL040000 SELF-HELP / Communication & Social Skills
PSY017000 PSYCHOLOGY / Interpersonal Relations

Cover Design by David Steele

Empowered Whole Being Press
www.EmpoweredWholeBeingPress.com

Note To The Reader: Community, Communication, Compassion

Alone I did not write this book. It bloomed out of me by my devotion to the Compassionate Communication community I serve. Were it not for this community and the many rich relationships I have within it, I could never have mustered the effort to produce these pages. My desire to enrich life, to touch and be touched by people I care about, drew forth the words herein.

We were initially drawn together by a shared respect for the Nonviolent Communication (NVC) work pioneered by Marshall Rosenberg, PhD. This is not an NVC book per se and does not require a working knowledge of NVC. It is heavily imbued with the insights and perspectives revealed by studying Marshall's work, however.

Unexpected Treasure

I have long heard how valuable a good editor is. I understood the meaning of those words, but the knowledge has been abstract until now. To bring this book into being, the collaboration between Laura Kennedy and myself has been nothing short of extraordinary! Without her editorial insight and diligence there would be no book. Often we look afar into some distant land or future time for the treasure we seek. The unexpected treasure living right in my neighborhood has proven far more valuable than anything I dared hope for!

Thank you, Laura!

Foreword

You are in for a treat, dear reader. David Steele has invited us on a tour of the human condition that feels as easy to take as a short walk with a friend.

In our half century of friendship, David and I have taken our share of walks, and I have learned something of how his mind works. He is a student of human psychology, math, politics, meditation, and pretty much everything else. He is a poet and a teacher of Compassionate Communication, a process for resolving conflict and developing healthy relationships by using self-awareness and skillful language. His fundamental attitude is curiosity.

In this volume, he brings us a few dozen essays, or meditations, that travel the ways of humanity, ways both meandering and coherent, both deadly serious and playful.

What could be more satisfying or more urgent than to explore what it is to be human? Whether we are checking for monsters under the bed or harnessing the power of nuclear fission, we must come to terms with the frightful power of human imagination, a power that is both fanciful and real.

David's longest course of study has been the cultivation of awareness, and he brings to these outings the eye of a trained observer. When he looks at our deeply polarized political moment, he sees it from a rare vantage point of genuine empathy for both sides. When he looks back at a formative experience like getting in trouble for sneaking off school grounds in the second grade, he brings a vivid recall coupled with a mature understanding.

Weaving through these vignettes and binding them together are the perennial questions – what is truth; what makes a fulfilling life; how do we go about building trust and community and a better world?

In this book, those questions reveal their common threads. As the feminist axiom goes, the personal is political; and, in this book, vice versa. Transforming big systemic power dynamics is linked with transforming our own consciousness.

Easier said than done, but David has some approachable suggestions for how to do it. The book is a call for us to do the work it takes to be more present, to ourselves and to each other.

In a clear and gentle voice, David is inviting us to grow up: to own the impact we each have on others whose lives we touch every day; to take responsibility for the fast-growing god-like powers we have as an endlessly clever species that has conquered our world.

Not only because the survival of countless humans and other sentient beings depends on it, but because it is our deep desire and higher destiny, because there is no greater challenge, and we are up to the challenge. And what could be sweeter than that?

Seth Henry
Longmont, Colorado

Table Of Contents

Part 3: Empathy

Introduction

I camped on a mountain top in my early 20s. For three weeks I meditated, attuned to nature, and pondered awareness. Those three weeks have reverberated through my life to this day. The day before I left my mountain top sanctuary, a voice in my head clearly spoke:

"Sure David, you have obtained an extraordinary level of consciousness, but you were in a sequestered environment with no responsibilities and all of your food prepared in advance. Now, return to the city and take up your life. If you can reach this level of consciousness amid the tumult of daily living responsibilities, then you can claim to have truly attained it."

This has proven no easy task. I attended numerous intensive trainings. I spent time in therapy and generally steeped myself in the human potential movement. I studied T'ai Chi Ch'uan, psychology, physiology, politics, philosophy, religion, mathematics, physics, metaphysics, mythology, and mysticism. Have I regained the extraordinary level of consciousness I experienced on the mountain top? No. Have my efforts to do so improved my life? Tremendously!

The rubber meets the road when we start translating insight from the sequestered, rarefied environment of the meditation retreat or the pages of an inspiring book to the omnipotently present economic, health, and relationship pressures that fill our lives. This book is for those devoted to "walking the talk" with the perseverance and determination such a path requires. Therefore, I use specific examples from my life and from society to concretely illustrate abstract principles and demonstrate how the abstract and concrete interact.

This book, based on a series of blogs I have written over the last four years, strives to shine light into darkness, not in an effort to call out or to simply illuminate, but in order to offer the warmth and accompaniment, the vitality, that light brings. There may be descriptions and language in these pages that some find troubling (consider this your trigger warning). I have done nothing to embellish or glorify them, nor have I attempted to tone down and sugar-coat them. I use the words and images I do because they accurately report what arises in my awareness. It has long been said that before you can accomplish something, you must first conceive of it. I choose the examples I do in the hope that I can spark a vision, a way forward, that is steeped in cooperation and inclusion, not contention and division.

The last few decades have seen a revolution in consciousness. We understand the human brain as never before. Physiological understanding has exploded. Wisdom-tradition insights have propagated; self-help and steps-to-enlightenment systems proliferated. Empowerment and manifestation is one of the seminal resonances of our day.

When it comes to grappling with the urgent challenges that humanity faces, the question arises: Do these resonances hold pragmatic value or are they a form of self-absorption that has no relevance to our current social issues?

Our dominion over the planet has become so omnipotent that the major threats to our well-being are born of the human imagination, not imposed by nature.

Can our consciousness, the source of our dominion, employ the wisdom to wield it? I am certain the answer is YES!

However, action directed purely out of calculation is inadequate; the complexities are simply too great. Thought alone cannot solve our dilemmas, nor can thought be discarded. We need a cooperation of the self, integrating the many aspects of our being, including both the word-bound and the wordless. We live in the time of the swarm, the time of leaderless movements and "lone wolf" actors. Roboticists were not able to get drones to mimic the flight of birds until they realized controlling the flock as a whole was impractical. The secret, they discovered, was to program individual drones to move autonomously and focus only on maintaining their relationship to the drones in their immediate vicinity.

The most complex technology we know is nature and the ecosystems that grow from it. Whether it is the atom at the core of the molecule, the molecule in the cell, the cell in the organ, or the organ in the body, each level plays the role for which it is suited: Thus, the organism thrives. Just as the flock of birds or swarm of drones maintains coherence by attending to its immediate surroundings.

Folk singer Pete Seeger was well known for saying, "Think globally, act locally."

Life is lived locally; that is where our actions have influence. Just as with the flock, by cultivating autonomy and attending to our close relationships do we build rich and fulfilling lives. These personal relationships form the ecology from which society and culture bloom. We can become gardeners, cultivators of relationships that grow a nourishing and wonderous reality.

What sunlight is to plants, presence is to relationships. Relationships thrive when we bring our attention to them and acknowledge that they matter. This is the essential survival skill our times demand: Being present. Our technological dominion amplifies our actions so quickly and so powerfully that haphazard behavior can threaten our very existence. Relationship is fundamental to existence. From the ground we stand on to the food we eat, from the microbe to the mountain top, our identity is the culmination of all of our relationships. Being present to our relationships, noticing where our awareness goes and what it delivers to our consciousness, gives us choice so that we can act purposefully. This leads us into discovery of who we are.

The same life that expresses through the ecosystem expresses through our consciousness. It possesses wisdom far beyond the capability of our intellect to grasp. When we reside in that wisdom, we experience a care and continuity that calculation and planning alone cannot provide.

We experience trust.

When we trust, we welcome life, we become comfortable with the intellect's inability to orchestrate it; the compulsion to micro-manage our existence dissipates. We express spontaneously, without pretense or expectation.

We practice authenticity.

Authenticity frees up tremendous amounts of energy. We feel lighter, more vital, and our attention, freed from micro-management, begins to explore. We become curious and adventurous. Our awareness moves outwards, no longer so focused on the self. We commune with the life that animates our very being, and we realize that even while we are autonomous individuals we are not separate … we share a common life essence.

We discover empathy.

Empathy reveals that common essence, makes us visible one to another. It connects us to nature and even the cosmos. When we reside in empathy, we can't help but want to contribute. We see how our own well-being is directly connected to global well-being. We deliberately participate in that one life that expresses through us and expresses through our environment. When we are present, we embody the wisdom that grows the ecosystem, and we discover what is ours to do just as the organ in the body knows what it is to do. Thus, we thrive, society thrives, the planet thrives.

Trust, authenticity, and empathy awaken us to who we are and reveal our individual and our human destiny. They light the path that leads us out of confusion and into meaning. They are the urgent calling of our times. Our continued well-being, even our survival, depends on following the path they illuminate.

Part One

Trust

Tho I be but one small person
I give part of myself to everyone I meet,
As much as I am able to offer
And they to accept,
And I gain part of them,
And we are both stronger,
And together we shape our world.

A Crossroads

We are at a crossroads. It is a crossroads we have encountered many times. At some level it is a crossroads we perpetually encounter, but our technological prowess now presents an urgency we have never faced. On July 16, 1945, at 5:20 am in the high plains between the towns of Carrizozo and Socorro, New Mexico, the first atomic explosion on Earth was detonated. In that instant humanity transformed; we harnessed the power of the stars and acquired the means to annihilate ourselves. Since that first nuclear test, named Trinity, the ways we can visit devastating harm upon ourselves have multiplied and currently include chemical, biological, and cyber technologies, not to mention global climate change.

Yet, all of these threats are born of the human imagination and the ingenuity with which that imagination sculpts the physical world. We are immensely powerful and resilient beings. Advances in medicine and food production have extended life expectancy. The worldwide standard of living is the highest it has ever been. Electricity runs refrigerators, and food does not spoil. Furnaces protect homes from freezing cold. Education, once the purview of a privileged few, is now readily available. Thanks to the internet, we can view the world through our computer screens and converse across continents on our smart phones.

Amid all of this complexity, how do we guide ourselves? How do we navigate the onslaught of information bombarding our senses, vying for our attention? How do we know where to place our trust? How do we discern the truthful from the deceptive and cultivate a secure reality that nourishes us?

If we cannot come up with satisfactory answers to these questions, we risk being devoured by fear and insecurity. Deeply exploring and answering these questions encourages a world of secure abundance and playful exuberance.

So, we arrive at our crossroads: Do we summon a reality driven by fear and loneliness or a reality held in love and compassion? This book is devoted to exploring that choice.

Truth

Truth can be defined as what our senses deliver to our awareness, conveyed through our nervous system, filtered by our brain, expressing as perception.

No one is willing to deny the evidence of their own senses. What we perceive simply feels right, and we experience it as real while the very cells in our bodies cry out in agreement. When we begin to doubt our own perceptions, we are beset by insecurity and paralysis because we are not sure we can trust our decisions. Perceptions are at the core of our identity, the fundamental experience "I Am." To doubt them is to doubt our very existence; it feels like annihilation. When someone endeavors to convince us that our perceptions are wrong or misguided, this will likely engage a fight, flight, freeze reaction as our physiology rallies to our defense. Conversely, when our perceptions are affirmed we feel secure and relaxed, because we no longer have to devote attention to protection. Our perspective expands, our ability to choose how we interact increases, and we gain a sense of ease and freedom. We trust our environment.

The human brain gets bombarded by billions of bits of information every minute. A minuscule portion of that information is sent up to the brain's higher processing regions. A lot of what the brain does is discard input it deems irrelevant. Research has shown that what is deemed relevant and irrelevant varies from person to person; that different brains filter things differently. We call this implicit bias. Consequently, two people can witness the same event and have entirely different descriptions of it, each sincerely convinced their description is the true and accurate one. This presents a dilemma for the justice system; it has been demonstrated that eye-witness testimony is not as omnipotently reliable as we once assumed.

This implies that truth is relative and depends on perspective. Relative perspective is the basic tenet of Einstein's mathematical Theory of Relativity and led directly to unlocking the core of the atom and our emergence into the nuclear age. Discovering that perspective can be relative while remaining truthful has an impact on human society that is every bit as profound as nuclear physics. We grapple with it to this day, especially with the advent of social media.

Consistency is essential to human well-being. We yearn for a common frame of reference where we can share experience, connect, and trust. We yearn for a stable reality supported by incontrovertible universal truth — truth affirmed by our community -- we set out to convince. Much of the violence and strife in the world arises from groups actively working to assert their relative perspective upon one another. Pope Benedict XVI called relative truth "the most profound difficulty of our time."

When we lived in smaller isolated communities, the relative nature of truth was less apparent. It was easy for the prevailing local worldview to permeate the community, while differing views seemed trivial and easily dismissed. With global communication and travel this is no longer possible. I remember the Vietnam War in the 1960s when the North Vietnamese were commonly referred to as "gooks," basically considered more animal than human. When we went to war in Iraq in 2003, President George W. Bush stated that we did not have any complaint with the

Iraqi people: Our complaint was with the Iraqi government. What a profound shift! We cannot so easily vilify an entire people anymore, thanks to our global connectedness.

Still, we tend to live in communities isolated one from another. As 2016 drew to an end, between the election of Donald Trump and his inauguration as president, a dear friend confided in me that she was waking up trembling with fear after dreaming that Trump launched a nuclear war. It reminded me of someone else who confided in me, his voice quivering with emotion, that he was ready to take up arms to defend the Constitution if Hillary Clinton won, because he feared she would immediately suspend the Second Amendment and institute a fascist government. I considered both of these people friends, well-meaning and considerate. Yet, the information filtering through their nervous systems and registering in their awareness was vastly different. They lived in entirely different communities with different histories, world views, mythologies, and assumptions about the nature of reality.

In the case of my friends, when their communities collided in the form of the election it was either traumatic or exhilarating, depending on your frame of reference. Many people, when they listen to Donald Trump, hear strength, resolve, authenticity, and they feel safety and relief. Others hear deception, intimidation, manipulation, and they feel fear and worry. Though my two friends had different reactions to the presidential election, what struck me was the fear. They were both reacting strongly to fear. In fact, fear was the reality they shared.

We all know what it is like to be scared, or to find joy, or to feel grief. Incontrovertible truth does exist. It is found in our bodies where we directly experience the beating of the heart, the teardrop in the eye, the emptiness when a dear one dies, the exhilaration when we greet a newborn. It is found in the nourishment that food delivers to our cells, in the tug of gravity that holds us to the Earth, in our need for sleep, in the rhythm of our breath.

R. Buckminster Fuller, inventor of the geodesic dome and one of the towering geniuses of the 20th century, lost his 4-year-old daughter to illness when he was 27. He became particularly distraught when he discovered there was a known cure, but the information had not yet been distributed through the medical community. He went on a four-year bender, drinking himself into unconsciousness every night. He had another daughter at age 31 and resolved to stop drinking. He made a deal with God: "If you help me stop drinking, I will devote my life to serving humanity."

It worked.

When he stopped drinking, he realized that he repeated things he heard as if they were true when he did not know, in fact, whether they were true or not. This troubled him greatly, and he decided to speak only of things as true that arose from his direct experience. However, he discovered that the habit of repeating unobserved things as true was so ingrained that he took a one-year vow of silence to break it: Thus, began his path to global impact. In one of the greatest understatements of all time, he said, "Of course, this was very hard on my wife."

I endeavor to follow Buckminster Fuller and use situations from my own life when teaching and convey what I have observed without assuming that I know the motivation that drives another's action or understand the way they perceive events. This posture allows me to have heartful conversations with people who fear that Donald Trump will launch a nuclear war or that Hillary Clinton will suspend the Second Amendment. I am far more interested in connecting than convincing.

Stripping away all details, circumstances, and ideologies, I ask myself, "Am I acting out of fear or out of love?" The answer to this question is substantially more important to me than whether someone is for gun rights or universal health care. If we are acting out of fear, the likelihood of violence increases. If we are acting out of love, creative solutions are likely to emerge. To quote Mahatma Gandhi, "Let us become the change we seek in the world."

Picking Apples

When I was in second grade, three classmates and I snuck into a field adjoining our playground to pick apples. We would go into that field with adult supervision to tend the class garden, but we were not to go there by ourselves.

We were spotted and brought before a teacher. "What were you doing in the field?" she asked the first of us. "I don't know," he replied. "Go sit in the hall until recess is over," he was told. The second one of us was asked the same question with the same result.

I was the third to be asked. I wanted to tell the truth, but I was scared. I opted for safety and gave the "I don't know" answer. As I was heading to the hall, the last of us, Sasha, was asked. "Picking apples," she confessed. "Thank you for telling the truth," the teacher said. "You may go back outside and play."

I remember being really mad at myself. I had wanted to tell the truth, really I did, but I couldn't summon the courage to deviate from the answer my peers gave. Sasha summoned that courage, and she got to return to the playground. If she had been asked before me, I am sure her example would have inspired me to tell the truth also. It was such a vivid lesson that I remember it to this day, long after most of second grade has dissolved into the mists of time. I even remember Sasha's name. We never know what impact our examples set.

Just Right

We love to plan. Could you go a week without looking at your calendar? Many of us draw comfort from our plan. Knowing what is going to happen next offers security. Sometimes we get so caught up in the plan and our determination to ensure it goes smoothly that we fail to notice what is unfolding right now and how the plan fits the present moment. When the present moment does not align with the plan we often feel stress, and we try to control what is happening in an effort to return to the plan; we become attached to outcome and endeavor to control events. This is a form of power over, of domination. How many of you have tried to control someone else's behavior in an attempt to fix a relationship or make yourself feel better? Maybe you try to change yourself to make them feel better. Is your self-talk full of phrases like, "If only they realized… If only they would… If only I had… If only I was… "?

We are often driven to try and orchestrate our external experiences as we search for security and safety. If only we can say just the right thing, know just the right information, put just the right people in office, buy just the right clothes, belong to just the right club, be seen at just the right event, then everything will be OK. However, life continually mutates and innovates. The future cannot be accurately predicted. The unexpected cannot be anticipated. The world is simply too complex and diverse to control.

Clinging to control, trying to compel how people behave and what should happen is ultimately a doomed endeavor.

In 2019, Denver held a mayoral run-off election. The contender, Jamie Giellis, could not recall what NAACP stood for at an event on May 15. This slip generated a lot of press, and she endured much criticism. The election went to the incumbent, Michael Hancock. At age 42, Giellis was born in 1977, well after the civil rights era. I have asked several people what NAACP stands for, and many of them did not know. How many of you reading this know? I would wager that those of you who do know lived through the civil rights movement or know a lot about it or grew up in an African-American cultural context.

We are living in a time of dramatic change and uncertainty. This naturally amplifies our urge to control and make things "just right," especially if we experience the world as a hostile, dangerous place. However, "just right" means very different things to different people. Thus, arises the divisiveness and polarization that currently consumes so much of our cultural expression.

Strangely, we have already become masters at controlling much of our external environment. From the taming of fire, including harvesting electricity; to climate control that protects us from fluctuations in weather; to engineered food supplies that feed billions and free most of us from the time and effort required to grow, hunt, and harvest food; to flying airplanes and driving cars; to staying continually connected with our smart phones; we hold dominion over much of our physical world. This has alleviated a huge amount of the toil staying alive requires, but it does not guarantee happiness or fulfillment, nor does it automatically diminish our urge to control.

All of these innovations that support our dominion over the planet have originated in the human consciousness and imagination. Ultimately, it is our consciousness and imagination that have relieved us of so much of life's toil and suffering. The power to cultivate security and safety also resides within us, not in our external environment. Giving up the urge to control requires that we learn to trust rather than tinker with ourselves. We cannot build trust with one we do not know. Knowing yourself is the first critical step in building the trust-that enables us to let go of attachment to outcome so that our well-being is not dictated by which definition of "just right" is currently popular.

Fear In The Park

When I was in my late 20s, I was throwing Frisbee with a couple of friends on a warm summer night. We were in a park near my house, standing under a streetlight. The park closed at 11:00 p.m., and it was well past midnight. A police car rolled up. We stopped and walked over to the waiting policeman. "We know, we know, the park is closed. We're leaving," I said. The policeman was calm and cool. As we headed out he explained, "we got a call from a woman claiming there was a gang fight going on in the park." We were stunned. There were only three of us, we had not been particularly loud, and the noise we made was more likely to be laughter than anything else. We certainly were not yelling. What kind of world, I wondered, did the caller live in where she perceived our low-key Frisbee game as a gang fight?

Several summers later, a friend was having marital problems. She came to stay with my girlfriend and me for a month. Not wanting to intrude, she set up her fold-out couch in our garage, making a cozy bedroom. Near the end of her stay, my girlfriend called me in a panic. "There are prowlers walking in our back yard," she exclaimed. I told her to call 911 and headed home. When I arrived, all was calm. It turned out that a neighbor had called the police to inform them we were running a meth lab out of our garage! The "prowlers" turned out to be the narcotics squad. They apologized and went on their way.

Police officers have a difficult job.

In both of these cases, I am guessing the callers lived in a fear-inundated world bereft of safety, where danger lurked, ever ready to nab them; a world where they responded to images and explanations that existed in their imaginations more than their physical surroundings. Yet, these imaginings, I am sure, induced strong physiological reactions in their bodies.

We humans are blessed with imagination. It is so potent it can obscure the physical reality surrounding us.-In many ways, imagination is more real than the physical world and gives us tremendous dominion over it. Yet, we cannot escape the laws of physicality that rule our body-bound existence. If we don't eat, we die.

When our imaginations work in concert with the physical world we are immensely powerful and potent. This is the essence of science. We focus on physicality and observe its behavior. We then use our imaginations to derive explanations for that behavior and render it coherent. We call these explanations "theories." We further use our imaginations to develop physical experiments that test our theories. Based on the results of the experiments, we affirm our explanations or again enlist our imaginations to further refine our theories to better fit the observed behavior. This interplay between imagination and observed physical manifestation produces understanding. It is called the scientific method and has liberated us from mass epidemics, given us smart phones, and produced lights that go on with the flip of a switch.

Foundational to the scientific method, observation is also a core and liberating principle of Nonviolent Communication. In the two police incidents described earlier, I suspect the fear the callers felt so inundated the foreground of their awareness that they were unable to clearly observe what was happening, so they jumped to conclusions.

Often in relationships we do the same thing. Fear or anxiety arise so powerfully that our imaginations move to the foreground, and we respond more to our internal explanations and expectations than to the actual dynamic flesh-and-blood person before us. We jump to conclusions about the intention behind their actions and the meaning of their statements. This often leads to anger and argument.

If we can take a minute to pause and observe what is going on, it creates a spaciousness that allows us to step back from our imagination and engage with our physical senses and sensations. Just like the scientist who develops theories, we can become curious: curious about why we are reacting the way we are; curious about what is going on with the other person. This curiosity often facilitates insight, our fear abates, and our actions reflect conscious deliberation instead of unconscious reaction.

Taking a breath and noticing what is going on in our bodies is an effective way to interrupt our automatic patterning and create that observational spaciousness. "My throat feels constricted and it aches, and my breathing is shallow. Wow, I am feeling a lot of confusion right now, and I want to yell. I wonder what that's about?" Such observational pausing integrates our imagination and our physical reality so we can become alert, open, and aware. This alertness often leads to exploration and discovery, and ultimately to understanding. Fear and anxiety move toward the background of our awareness, the person we are interacting with becomes more visible and vivid, and we are able to cultivate cooperation and partnership.

Security begins with feeling safe, feeling that we can trust our world. When nameless fear and anxiety mount, try reconnecting to your physical world by observing what is going on in your body and how you are experiencing the present moment … become curious.

Relief and understanding will likely emerge.

Fear In The Basement

At age 6, I moved with my family into a new house, one with a basement. I was afraid to go into that basement, because I thought a man with a butcher knife lived down there and he would get me. No amount of reasoned argument or assurance could convince me to go down those steps alone. When accompanied by my mother, however, the basement was a fun place. By the time I was a teenager, I lived in that basement, my personal refuge from an encroaching adulthood that I viewed with trepidation.

Whether it's the boogie man in the closet or the monster under the bed, we have all gone through times when we were haunted by nameless fears that no amount of logic could banish. However, when someone pauses and listens to those nameless fears they tend to diminish. When a parent looks under a bed with us to check for monsters, the fear becomes manageable. When our experience is welcomed, we feel less alone. In contrast, when we are told our fears are crazy or irrational, insecurity mounts. We begin to doubt our own perception. Loneliness increases, and we tend to perceive the world as hostile.

When one is haunted by fear, accompaniment provides a powerful source of strength and solidarity. When others acknowledge and share our fear, we gain a sense of assurance, affirmation, even vindication. This dynamic underlies many unlikely yet fervently held beliefs such as "global warming is a hoax designed to trick us into surrendering our sovereignty to the U.N.," or "there is a Muslim plot to take over the U.S. county by county and institute Sharia law."

While I may not subscribe to these perspectives, millions of people do. They take comfort when they discover others who share their perceptions, plus they find plenty of internet articles that affirm their position. They can also enjoy the thrill of being someone "in the know" who can see the truth while others are blind, or who has the courage to speak the unspeakable.

We now understand how essential accompaniment is to our physiological well-being. Our brains are hard wired to seek ways to belong, to be an accepted member of the tribe. This is one of the most prominent drives propelling our teenage lives. It is the foundation that supports fads and underpins advertising. The urge to "keep up with the Joneses" is enticing … no one wants to be left out.

When I was a little kid, the basement was not scary when my mother was there; it was only terrifying when I was alone. This illustrates the power of belonging. When we know that we are accompanied, we become courageous and devoted. Our lives assume greater meaning. Fear still impacts us, but it does not control us.

Participating in social trends contributes to a shared reality that gives us something to talk about with friends and in social settings, especially when we are new to a community. As our social connections deepen and we find a place where we belong — a place "where everybody knows your name" — we will fiercely defend that community. Just as we have become a part of it, it has become a part of us.

I have no fear that the U.S. will surrender its sovereignty to the U.N., but I understand the importance of sovereignty and one's fierce desire to guide one's own destiny. Muslims taking over the country does not seem plausible to me, but I understand devotion to a way of life that affirms one's existence, providing solace amid difficulty; I understand one's resolute determination to protect that way of life.

The next time you meet someone you disagree with or hear something in the news that distresses you, can you become curious and adventurous instead of fearful and angry? Can you wonder, "what is going on that someone would say or believe such a thing?"

Constantly Bombarded

We live in an increasingly fragmented, or perhaps I should say fractal, world. Choose your reality and endlessly explore. From nanotechnologist to earthquake researcher, from geo-political analyst to county commissioner, we have never before had to choose from such a vast array of options.

Choices abound. Recently, I went to buy hand soap and was confronted with choice upon choice upon choice. I remember a time when there were six or seven options, each a different brand. Now one brand alone has six or seven nuanced choices. There must have been 30 or 40 options all told. Don't even ask how many salsa options I had!

These myriad options vie for our attention. We are constantly bombarded with sights and sounds asking us to notice and embrace them. According to a training I took from educator Jean Houston, the density of stimulation bombarding our nervous system has increased more than 10-fold in the last 100 years. We have no idea how this is impacting our brains since we have no brain tissue from a century ago for comparison. What we do know is that our brains are changing.

One of these changes, I believe, is that we have forgotten silence and how profoundly it contributes to inner equilibrium and hones our attention. When we are constantly reacting to aggressive stimuli, it is easy to lose track of who we are or even remember that we are.

An exercise in a workshop I was conducting generated such enthusiasm that it went well over its allotted time. A participant was sharing their insight during the group discussion following the exercise. Meanwhile, my mind was filled with thoughts about how I would adjust the lesson plan to accommodate running overtime. I heard the participant's words, but they were distant in my awareness, unable to penetrate the thoughts I was having. The participant stopped speaking and I realized, to my dismay, I had no idea what they had just said. To cover, I asked them to repeat their point using slightly different words. This time, alert and present, their words easily made sense to me.

Effective communication begins with listening, and listening is based in silence. For me, one tell-tale indication that I am out of balance is when I start talking to myself while someone else is speaking. When I can quiet myself and go into silence, their presence registers more vividly in my awareness, and I feel a deeper connection with them. They sense the connection, and our conversation becomes more meaningful and satisfying.

One of the profound benefits of cultivating silence and deepening our ability to listen is that we become more aware of and connected to ourselves. This increases our level of security and confidence. When we become more aware of our own needs and listen to the various voices within us, we experience authenticity, integrity, and courage. Life becomes more fun, our relationships become more fulfilling, and our ability to create the world we want to live in becomes more potent. Practice being silent and listening: Prepare to be amazed and delighted!

Put Your Heart Into It

We have all heard the phrase "put your heart into it." I have always understood this to mean that you can accomplish more, produce a higher quality, and have a rich meaningful experience when your heart is involved. We somehow grasp that our hearts are a source of tremendous energy. Movies that touch our hearts get awards. Politicians strive to touch our hearts and win our votes. I have long been amazed at how much more energy flows through my body when my heart is into a project. If my heart is not in something, I sometimes have to force myself to do it in a mechanical way, eager for it to be over.

A barrage of 50th anniversary programs commemorating the moon landing appeared this summer. Barely a teenager when Apollo 11 landed on the moon on July 16, 1969, I was an avid follower of the space program and watched the grainy live landing images with rapt attention. Viewing some of the 50th anniversary programs, I found myself moved to tears. You might say they "stirred my heart." I felt vividly alive and grateful as these retrospectives touched me.

Going to the moon is an example of what we can accomplish when we "put our hearts into it." The heartfelt energy we tapped was partly rooted in a fear that the Soviets would dominate space with nuclear weapons and possibly destroy us. There was also the sense of adventure that exploration evokes. And there was the exhilaration that comes from solving problems and overcoming obstacles. Then there was the suspense, the challenge, the ambition: What will happen next? Can we pull it off?

The space program that culminated in the lunar landing is an excellent example of the heart and the mind working together to animate the body in a massively cooperative endeavor, comprised of individual effort, that produced a deep sense of pride and camaraderie. The result was spectacular! Thousands of people, dozens of companies, and multiple government bureaucracies had to work together and communicate effectively, coordinating hundreds of thousands of details, spanning years. If our hearts were not in it, we could not have mustered the perseverance and money required to pull it off. If our minds had been distracted and preoccupied, we would never have solved the technical problems. If our communications were guarded and deceptive, with each company and individual jockeying for personal advantage, it would have crumbled into chaos. Hearts and minds had to come together and then communicate effectively in service to a shared vision.

Heartfelt presence provides a sense of authenticity and aliveness that the mind alone simply cannot produce. Yet, without the tempering influence of the mind, the heart can act blindly and destructively. Heart provides us with connection, belonging, participation in our world. Mind gives us individuality, autonomy, and the ability to shape our world. When combined, heart and mind enable us to make manifest our deepest selves and bring true our dreams. Communication makes visible those dreams, enabling us to share them and give them life so that the body can bring them into the physical world. Everything we create is inspired by the heart, directed by the mind, and brought into being by the body.

Thus, we have impact and know that our presence matters.

When the mind learns to trust and the heart learns to dance, the body is filled with vitality. Abundance and joy become our constant companions, and gratitude flavors our every experience!

Woodstock

This year marks the 50th anniversary of Woodstock. In 1969 I was old enough to know it was going on, but too young to attend. Whatever you may think of it, it left an indelible mark on the American psyche.

I came of age in the early 1970s with deep roots in the hippie movement of the 1960s.

I perceived Woodstock as an amazing example of how people can spontaneously get together, be creative, and help each other: a shining testament to the human spirit. I have heard other people, with sincere passion, call it an example of debauchery and immorality. Initially I was oblivious to this perspective. As it continued to assert itself, I dismissed it as misguided or propaganda. Only decades later, after I watched retrospective documentaries on the 1960s, was I willing to truly pay attention. Many conservative thinkers called Woodstock the worst thing that had ever happened to our culture: Revelers exhibited disrespect for authority, publicly used foul language, and had no moral restraint. Many conservatives seem to sincerely believe Woodstock marked the beginning of a descent into depravity that will destroy our civilization.

Any coherent society is maintained by a moral code that guides behavior. I perceived Woodstock as a shining testament to the human spirit because I was operating from a different moral code than many conservative thinkers were, with different basic assumptions about human nature. I am sure my moral code was as invisible to them as theirs was to me. Both codes bring coherence, even if they seem to be at odds. I admit, it took a lot of listening and questioning the validity of my own basic assumptions before I could see the life-serving purpose in their perspectives.

Woodstock has never been repeated. The next attempt, Altamont, was inundated with shysters out to make a quick buck. Violence erupted; four people were killed.

The liberal church youth group that I belonged to in the early 1970s experimented with encounter groups, crafted youth-directed education, consciously explored sexuality, and questioned authority. We were opposed to the Vietnam War and did not trust our government. It was not a comfortable group to belong to at times and was monitored by the FBI. As fringe positions became mainstream, I watched the youth group implode. In the mid-1970s people joined simply to be cool, party, get laid, and do drugs. It was the same trajectory that led from Woodstock to Altamont.

I have now seen this trajectory many times and think of it as the Woodstock Effect. I was on the internet before there were spam and viruses, and when I first joined Facebook the focus was on connecting with friends without having to boost posts.

My mother, born in 1917, once told me she did not feel at home in our culture until the 1960s. She liked to dance to rock-and-roll and eat unprocessed food. I remember her anger when she discovered, in 1960, that she could not apply for credit simply because she was a woman. Mail arrived addressed to Mrs. Don Robert Steele, her late husband's name.

We deliberately moved to Denver's Park Hill in the early 1960s because she wanted me to grow up in a racially and economically integrated neighborhood. She was an outspoken proponent of civil rights.

Thanks to changes wrought in the 1960s, I can buy peanut butter made only of peanuts and salt, and organic fresh food is readily available (at least in Denver). Recycling has become integrated into our daily lives, rivers no longer catch on fire because of the chemicals dumped into them, my view of the mountains is not obscured by a car exhaust haze, I enjoy collaborating with female colleagues in the workplace, birth control is readily available, and domestic violence is now recognized as a crime.

Today, as I consider the impact of climate change, or how we are poisoning the food chain with plastics, or the massive number of species extinctions underway, I wonder how we will survive. I am tempted by desperation and despair. After Donald Trump won the U.S. presidential election in 2016, as I watched his "American Carnage" inaugural speech, I felt a heavy dark constriction grip my body and wondered if I was witnessing the disintegration of our civilization.

After his victory, I often heard the comment, "Now you know how we felt for the last eight years."

If you grew up taking for granted that marriage is only between a man and a woman, that marijuana turns men into fiends, that a woman's place is in the home, and that white people are the natural rulers — and now you see prayer banned in schools, Merry Christmas replaced by happy holidays, birth control usurping God's will, and abortion as government-sanctioned murder, I have no doubt you feel a heavy dark constriction grip your body and you wonder if you are witnessing the disintegration of our civilization.

I live in a city with a low unemployment rate and rapid economic growth. I don't have first-hand experience of a largely deserted town square with boarded up shops. I have not lived in a city with block after block of vacant homes and factories. I don't know anyone who lost their farm to foreclosure. There is no opiate epidemic ravaging the circles I travel in.

Resonating with these perspectives, I can see how President Trump's talk about American carnage rings true.

I get it: "Now you know how we felt" is not just a catchy comeuppance. The distress I feel today is the same distress many felt eight years ago. Now I do know how they felt.

My attention is no longer drawn to left or right, right or wrong, liberal or conservative. What I see is human beings working hard to make sense of their world, provide for their families, and lead meaningful, dignified lives.

At the time of Woodstock there was a war raging in Vietnam, riots ravaged many of our cities, and the civil rights struggle was in full flower. The country had been stunned by political assassinations, buildings were being bombed by extremist groups, and we were told, "You can't trust anyone over 30."

In the midst of all this the human spirit revealed itself as half a million people shared three days of music on a remote farm in upstate New York with inadequate sanitation, food, and shelter. They looked after each other as best they could, sharing what they had while singing songs of peace.

I saw the same caring community spirit that characterized Woodstock emerge during the 2017 floods in Houston when people across the country spontaneously mobilized to look after one another. I experienced it first-hand at the birth of personal computing as companies and techies freely shared their time and expertise so we could learn to wield this incredible new tool. Most profoundly, I experienced it in my church youth group where we were accepted for who we were as together we explored what it meant to be human.

I am sure the spirit revealed at Woodstock has been with us all along. The earliest instance I know of in any detail was the Christmas truce of 1914 when British and German troops laid down their arms on Christmas Eve, sang carols together, played soccer, and shared stories and photographs of home. Soldiers on both sides were ordered not to talk about it and, according to the History Channel website, "it was never repeated — future attempts at holiday ceasefires were quashed by officers' threats of disciplinary action."

The Christmas truce is a testament to how strong the urge to connect and care is, and how much effort it takes to suppress it. Bubbling just beneath the surface, it is ready to emerge at any moment, is emerging at every moment, patiently waiting to see if we notice.

Sacred Duty

I tend to get a bit choked up around Memorial Day. I knew several Vietnam War vets and the struggles they faced. Although my father died when I was very young, he served in the army in the late 1940s. I still have the flag that draped the coffin at his military funeral. I know, although not closely, people who served in Iraq and Afghanistan. Soldiers are willing to kill and die in order to protect us. Without their devotion, we would have no country.

Often, soldiers refer to their service as a sacred duty. When they are killed, we call it the ultimate sacrifice. Why do we humans risk our well-being in service to others? Why do we deliberately endure hardship so they can prosper? How does sacrifice in service to those we love — or to principles that we hold dear — nourish and fulfill us, give our lives meaning? What are the rewards of parenting, of volunteering for a religious or civic institution, of helping our neighbors during a natural disaster? Is it not a sacred act whenever we put another's well-being in front of our own?

These questions so move me that I created a workshop called Sacrifice and Sacrament to explore them. Yet, "context is everything." When I talk about sacrifice and sacrament in the context of Memorial Day, I am guessing you feel deep resonance, and my words make sense. The first time I offered this workshop, it was an informal test run. One of the participants asked about my choice of words, Sacrifice and Sacrament. For her, this title evoked childhood memories of coercion and compulsion, of never being good enough no matter how hard she tried. To her, the phrase Sacrifice and Sacrament meant suffering, shame, guilt, and punishment. I was astounded by how my words landed with her, when their meaning was so clear and obvious to me. The meaning she found was grounded in her own experience, an experience I never had or even imagined. Yet, when she explained the basis for her reaction, it made total sense. When, on other occasions, I encountered similar reactions, I considered changing the name of the workshop. I have not yet found a replacement title that fits.

Words are containers. Just as a truck carries cargo and a car holds passengers, words convey meaning. Phrases like "What I am hoping to convey … " are common. Meaning arises from the intention behind our words. When you speak, what do you intend to convey? This intention is expressed by vocal intonation and body language as much as it is by the dictionary definitions of the words. Being clear on our intention helps ensure that the meaning our words carry is authentic and potent. When our intentions are not seen and the meaning derived from our words differs from what we expect, we can experience confusion, fear, or anger. When this happens to me, the intention behind my words shifts to a quest for understanding and shared reality. I much prefer this to arguing and convincing.

When we go to the doctor for a physical exam, they often tap our knee with a rubber mallet causing our foot to swing forward without any conscious volition: the knee-jerk reaction. Many of the words and phrases we encounter during political campaigns and in advertising are deliberately and skillfully designed to produce the psychological equivalent to the knee-jerk reaction. This tack can bypass our thoughts and intellect to produce a strong emotion that propels us into taking action without thinking about it or considering how it will impact others. Often these techniques are intended to induce punishment, ridicule, or blame as a means to dominate. Such interactions promote violence. When these situations arise, do we succumb to violence ourselves, spreading it like a virus? Or do we defuse it, acting as an antibody?

Learning how to recognize and manage our knee-jerk reactions to words is one of the urgent tasks before us. Our technology has grown so potent and amplifies our actions so powerfully that knee-jerk reaction imperils our species and planet.

When you speak, pause to consider the intention behind your words and the meaning you want to convey. When you experience that knee-jerk reaction ask yourself, "Why am I impacted so?" When someone ascribes a meaning beyond what you anticipated or even imagined, can you shift the intention behind your words to a quest for understanding and shared reality?

Nothing Artificial

Inventor R. Buckminster Fuller did not like the word "artificial." In his view, we cannot create anything that does not adhere to the laws of physics and chemistry. His concern was that the word artificial implies that humans are separate from nature and that this sense of separation enables us to damage and destroy the very environment that our lives depend on.

The largest volcanic eruption on which we have firm data happened in Iceland during 1783–1784. When Mt. Laki blew, 565 square miles were covered with ash. Sunlight was unable to reach the ground for months. Sulphur plumes displaced oxygen. All of the plants died. Soon after, all of the animals and humans starved to death. I live in a world where I can easily walk to a store and get something to eat in the middle of the night during a snowstorm. My senses report no imminent threat to my food supply, my safety seems secure.

We can go several weeks without food, several days without water, and only a few minutes without air. The perception that we are separate from the Earth is an illusion, a deadly illusion. As philosopher Alan Watts said, "We grow out of this Earth in much the same way an apple grows out of a tree." Without plants burrowing their roots into the soil and sending their photon collectors — leaves — into the sky, we would all be dead. Our survival is dependent on the sun, a nonstop thermonuclear reactor located a convenient 93 million miles away. Any closer and it would fry us; any farther away and we would freeze. The energy it releases provides the sustenance upon which all earthly life depends. Plants have learned how to store that energy in clusters of carbon and hydrogen. When we eat, our blood carries those carbohydrates to our cells where their captured energy is released, fueling our very existence.

Back in 1969, who would have predicted that the most profound impact resulting from our journey to the moon was the view of the Earth as seen from space? This visual sensory input drove home, as never before, the fact that there is only one Earth, that if we blow it here there is nowhere else to go. The emergence of a global identity began with those pictures of Earth from space. This marks when we first recognized that we do indeed live on "Spaceship Earth," as Buckminster Fuller liked to put it.

From snow lichen in the arctic tundra to microbes that cluster around thermal vents in the deep ocean floor, we find that life is endlessly versatile, adaptable, resilient, and innovative. This same life animates our body, regulates our breathing, and beats our heart. When we anchor our awareness in our aliveness, becoming present to the fact that we are, confidence and resourcefulness ensue. We feel secure, allow ourselves vulnerability, and participate in life. We recognize that the same aliveness that flows through us also flows through others and throughout nature: We experience connection and inclusion, our dependence on the Earth becomes vivid and wondrous, and we thrive.

There is little disagreement that our global situation is unsustainable, that we are in need of dramatic transformation. There is much disagreement about what that transformation should be and how best to accomplish it. How can we galvanize our efforts into coherent action that will effectively address our global challenges? Our current situation is the result of billions of individual and diverse decisions made each moment. Amid this chaotic immensity, what impact can one person have?

Decisions are made and actions taken by individuals. Change and transformation flows through us; we are all change agents. Remembering our connection to the Earth, our dependence on food, water, and air, provides an effective guide for our decisions. It brings coherence to our actions and provides a basis for us to pool our resources so that we can accomplish the truly miraculous. It reminds us that we must nurture our community so that our community can support us, that we are a part of the Earth every bit as much as it is a part of us. This insight galvanizes our efforts into action that will effectively address our global challenges.

There is nothing more powerful than life, and that very life resides within us. It resides within you!

Giving And Receiving

I was recently assisting with a Compassionate Communication class called Giraffe Talk for 2nd through 5th graders. We were playing a game about preferences called "This or That" where each participant would move, say, to the left if they liked cake or to the right if they liked ice cream. The game moved quickly through a variety of choices. One of the choices was "giver or receiver." What really struck me was that as the group started to split, the kids who were moving toward receiver noticed a majority of kids moving to giver and switched. I ended up being the only one to stand with receiver.

Why, at such an early age, did the children feel pressure to switch to giver? Why is being a giver perceived as being better than a receiver? Is it because receiving is considered selfish, putting your needs above someone else's, a form of domination? Is it because receiving is considered weak, a flaw whereby you cannot take care of yourself, a form of submission? Is it because we feel flawed and unworthy of kindness and gifts?

For someone to give, someone else must receive; likewise, for one to receive, someone else must give. Giving and receiving are the exhale and inhale of a single breath. When the breathing is balanced, we are healthy and enjoy a sense of well-being. Constantly giving is like trying to maintain one long exhale. Eventually we must inhale, but when we do so it will be because we are desperate and have no choice. Desperation and compulsion are the features often associated with receiving as a weakness. If giving and receiving were balanced, perhaps the perception of receiving as desperate and weak would vanish, and we would be able to accept gifts and acknowledgment with grace.

Which One Wins

November 2015: I am grateful to live in a society that devotes a day to gratitude. Yesterday was Thanksgiving, a day to reflect on what we have rather than what we lack. When we focus on what we have, the world is a much friendlier place.

My heart aches for the people whose lives have been rent asunder by hurricanes, floods, tornadoes, and fires this last year. My heart is warmed by the communities that rush to their aid from first responders who risk their lives, to craftsmen and volunteers who show up to help clean up and rebuild, to cooks and dishwashers who roll up their sleeves to run kitchens. There are the people who run shelters, who sort through shipments and help get resources to those who need them, and the people who coordinate raising money to support all of these efforts. Some of these people work for governments, some work for business, some work for nonprofits, and some are retired or self-employed. All contribute.

My heart aches as I think about the shooting at the Emanuel African Methodist Episcopal Church in Charleston, South Carolina, on June 17. Sad and horrifying as the event was, I am amazed by the outpouring of grief and solidarity from people of all colors, ages, and creeds. It is a sharp contrast from the 1990s when black churches were burned on a regular basis and — except for the

African American community — we, as a nation, hardly noticed. Looking back over decades, the transformation is stunning.

There is a consciousness revolution and evolution underway. It is moving fast. Invisible, yet potent, it makes for boring copy on the news so it remains invisible until the Berlin Wall crumbles or attitudes on gay marriage rapidly shift. I know people who look at the world in dismay and despair, feeling powerless, and understandably so. When I look at the world I see incredible beauty, strength, and resilience; a world deeply imbued with love.

As I write this, I am sitting in a warm comfortable room with electricity and food, a member of a community that welcomes me. My awareness is awash with gratitude. There are many everyday things that I find amazing and am thankful for. As an antidote to the turmoil and anxiety we are experiencing as a people, I thought I would highlight some. I am grateful for warm showers, for lights that turn on at the flip of a switch. Indoor plumbing is a favorite of mine. Toilet paper is an incredible invention that much of the world does not enjoy. Paved roads rank high on the gratitude scale as do grocery stores. I am grateful I can drive to the store on paved roads without having to worry about roadside bombs or snipers. I am grateful for my ancestors who worked hard to make all of this possible. I am grateful to have enough to eat and friends to share it with. I am grateful for the community I have. I am grateful when people show up at my trainings and when they read my essays. Most of all, I am grateful for life, precious and mysterious beyond my ability to express.

I am reminded of the timeless story about a youth who approaches a village elder. The youth asks, "How can you be so calm and peaceful? I feel a war within me where the darkness threatens to extinguish the light." The elder replies, "I too feel the darkness and the light at war, like two dogs locked in a vicious battle within me." Amazed, the youth asks, "Which one wins?" "Whichever one I feed the most," replies the elder.

Despair and powerlessness, or beauty and resilience? How much energy do you devote to each? Part of the transformation sweeping through our consciousness is the understanding of how our brains and stimulus-response physiology work and what we can do to break habitual patterns that imprison us.

It is possible to transform and summon that world of beauty and resilience. It takes dedication and perseverance, but the rewards are immense. Perpetual gratitude for instance.

Who Is Listening

Kittens pounce on imaginary objects. Puppies vigorously bite. Bear cubs wrestle and roll. When mammals are young they play, and that play hones the essential skills they need as adults. When young, children take on stories, playing nurse or policeman, superhero or mud-pie chef. Crafting story is the essential skill we humans must master as adults. The uniquely human ability to conjure story that makes sense of and brings meaning to our world is at the root of our tool-wielding ability, our artistic rendering of experience, our capacity to create culture. It enables us to dominate the planet. This stewardship comes with momentous responsibility to both understand ourselves and understand our environment.

We develop great allegiance to the stories that bring coherence to our world. They provide continuity and security. Without story our world becomes chaotic, and we cannot function. Story is so critical to our well-being that when we encounter inconsistencies in our story, we often perceive them as threats. In fact, much of the stress and anxiety we experience comes from trying to make our actual experience conform to the story we hold.

Stories are key to our identity, and we often use them to define who we are. However, when our sense of self does not extend beyond our stories, we are captive to them, victims of our descriptions and conditioning. So familiar is our story-spinning nature that we forget that every story requires an audience. There is a witness in each of us, silent and motionless. In much the same way a drawing begins with an empty page, the witness provides space for the story to emerge. You cannot have the drawing without the page, and you cannot have the story without the witness.

When you talk to yourself, who notices, who listens?

When our sense of self shifts from the story to the witness, our perspective changes. We experience the story as living within us rather than us living within the story. The story no longer fills our entire universe, and we experience ease and spaciousness. We are no longer the victim of our story: We become its author. Life reveals itself a creative adventure rather than an inescapable burden, suffering is replaced by joy, and we step into our potential as a human being: weaver of story, author of destiny. This is the fulfillment we are called to when, as children, we play nurse or policeman, superhero or mud-pie chef.

Freedom and empowerment lie in the stories we cleave to, in the descriptions that make sense of our lives. This book is itself an exploration into that power of narrative. The ability to entertain different, seemingly contradictory narratives and touch the truth and vitality in each is an exercise in trust, authenticity, and empathy. In the spirit of authenticity, I draw examples from world events, some of them traumatic; I trust in the reader's capacity to digest them; and I hope to demonstrate how empathy looks in practice. My tag line, "compassion is not for the faint of heart" applies here. By looking into darkness do we reveal the light hidden within and discover that love is ever present. Thus, can we mend the fissures that separate us one from another and assuage the torment our society is enduring.

Part Two

Authenticity

How tough is tough?
You got the right stuff?
Like guts
Guts enough to trust?
To live the love?
To open your heart
And let it sing?
Be true to yourself
And follow your dreams?
Just how courageous
Has your mind grown?
Do you even know
When your thoughts are your own
And when you're being spoon fed?
Are you filled with dogma?
Is there honesty inside?
Can you handle the truth?
Do you run and hide?
Are you a wimp?
Or are you a human being?

Which Face

At times I feel awash in grief over the divisiveness, blaming, and criticism that grips much of our country. The episode below illustrates why I feel grief at times. Looking back, I also think this was when the seed was planted for Standing Tall, a training that arose from my determination to do something about drawing strength from our own convictions in a way that enables us to listen fully to others and find deep wisdom in our mutual authenticity.

During the 2012 presidential race between Mitt Romney and Barack Obama, I was buying groceries at my little neighborhood store near Denver's City Park, where I had been shopping for years and felt some kinship with the owners. They worked very hard to keep their store afloat, and I wanted to support my community. While paying, I made an off-hand comment about the importance of voting. The owner, who was checking out my groceries, asked me if I supported Romney. My response was that I thought he would be a competent president.

The owner's face brightened, and she told me she was strongly supportive of him. She began to tremble as she explained that she had put up a Romney poster, and her customers began criticizing her. She could not keep the bitterness out of her voice as she explained that her customers started boycotting her store. "And I thought these people were my friends," she said. "This is my livelihood!" She took down the Romney poster, put up an Obama one, and hid her political views. "There is no way I would ever vote for a Democrat now," she proclaimed.

This was a woman who took the time to ask how my mother was doing, knowing I was caring for her. As my mother lost her mobility, she still loved to drive around with me. It gave her an opportunity to stay engaged with the neighborhood she had walked for decades. When I went shopping, the owner would leave her store, come out to the car, and engage my mother in conversation. As my mother's dementia grew to the point where she could not hold coherent conversations, the owner would still spend time talking with her. Even when my mother could not remember who this woman was, her face would light up with joy when she saw her.

This was the same woman standing across from me at the cash register, trembling with anger about having to pretend she was an Obama supporter. Hence, my grief.

These days I stand for compassion; all else is detail.

Today, we are putting so much attention on the battle, why I'm right and why you're wrong, that we become blind to what we dearly care about. We become willing to boycott the business of a deeply caring woman because she supports the "wrong" presidential candidate. Martin Luther King, Jr., famously spoke of a world where we do not judge others "by the color of their skin but by the content of their character." I would add "and not by the presidential candidate they support."

Have you ever watched footage of the civil rights marches of the 1960s inspired by Dr. King? When the camera pans the crowd, you see some faces filled with anger and hatred, screaming and yelling. The faces of the marchers show some fear, but they are also calm and silent. The marchers proceed resolutely, unflinchingly, forward into the sea of clamoring hatred surrounding them. I imagine their attention was on why they were there and what they stood for more than the surrounding hostility.

Today there are many demonstrations and intense social media discussions. Passions run deep. I think of my friend at the neighborhood market when I engage people who hold views that I find disturbing, and I think back to those faces from the civil rights marches and I ask myself: Which face do I show?

When you engage others in service to your passionate beliefs, which face do you show?

Do You Have The Courage

We are in the midst of profound, dramatic, and irresistible transformation. Epoch after epoch, like an unstoppable ocean surf, change relentlessly washes over us. We have lived through the industrial age, the space age, the computer age, the information age. I have heard that we live in the age of DNA and designer drugs, the age of robotics and nanotechnology, the age of the digital revolution with smart phones and social media. Or how about the age of brain imaging and neuroscience or the age of artificial intelligence? Most fundamentally, however, we live in the nuclear age, the age of weapons of mass destruction, the age of impending ecological catastrophe, the age when our technological prowess cannot be ignored.

It is no wonder we are inundated with stress and anxiety. Of course there is an upsurge of fear and a longing for the "good old days" and "traditional values." Do we endeavor to soothe this fear or to attack it? Soothing fear diminishes it, enabling us to think clearly and solve problems, while attack heightens fear and arouses blame. A liberal-leaning professor in Kansas was relegated to "desk duty" with no classes because she vigorously confronted a student advocating for a conservative cause. A conservative-leaning professor in Pennsylvania was stripped of most of her classes because she wrote a paper praising Western European values and was labeled a white supremacist. Liberal organizations point to the situation in

Kansas to demonstrate how horrible conservatives are. Conservative organizations point to the situation in Pennsylvania to demonstrate how horrible liberals are. It reminds me of two kids squabbling on the playground, both vehemently insisting it was the other person's fault, except that our national bickering could easily lead to bloodshed.

I remember the late 1960s and early 1970s. I did not like it when protesters called police officers pigs. I don't like it today when people call immigrants an infestation. When I approach a situation, I ask myself, "Are people guided by hatred and fear or are they guided by compassion and love?" From this perspective, the details become much less relevant. Details simply are; they can be used to stoke hatred and fear, or they can be used to evoke compassion and love.

For people who think compassion is a weakness, I ask:

- Do you have the courage to look someone you disagree with in the eye and see a living, breathing human being?

- Do you feel secure enough in your own life not to be threatened by world views that differ from yours?

- Do you have the humility to admit you don't have all the answers and then deeply listen?

- Are you willing to give up blame and being "right?"

- Can you accompany someone's suffering without looking away?

Compassion is not for the faint of heart. It requires tremendous courage, trust, and honesty. It also minimizes the likelihood of bloodshed and cultivates peaceful solutions without anyone having to surrender what they hold dear.

Sticks And Stones

As a child I learned the rhyme "sticks and stones can break my bones, but words can never hurt me." Nothing could be further from the truth. Words have a profound impact on how we sculpt our reality and the actions we take. They can set our inspirations free or imprison us in trauma.

On March 26, 2018, I listened to an interview on Colorado Public Radio exploring the relationship between mental health and violence. It turns out that mental health is a relatively minor factor but tends to make the news frequently. The interview was with Dr. Jason Williams, a pediatric psychologist associated with Children's Hospital Colorado, and Dr. Michael Allen, who teaches and practices psychiatry and emergency medicine and treats patients at the Depression Center of the University of Colorado Anschutz Medical Campus.

To address the root causes of violence, they were asked what one major change they would make if they could. They gave two responses. The first was screening kids for depression as a common practice, starting at age 10. Here follows their second response:

"You start talking about emotions as young as preschool, emotional literacy, and giving kids the opportunity to learn how to express themselves. You basically teach people to use verbal skills. It's true that among people who are violent, their verbal skills are less good than people who are not. You can train people to use words to solve problems, then violence goes down."

Communication skills are not a luxury. They are essential for the health of our society and planet as well as for our personal well-being. Deepening your own communication skill is something you can do to change the world that does not involve convincing, arguing, blaming, or becoming a political activist.

Footnote: One of my readers offered the following comment on an earlier version of this essay: "I quote the less-quoted platitude, 'Sticks and stones may break my bones but names will break my heart.'"

All Voices

Spring 2018: Like many the world over, I was horrified by the sounds and images coming from our southern border as migrant children were forcibly separated from their parents. Particularly difficult were the scenes of infants being ripped from their mothers' arms. Yet, such occurrences are nothing new to people who study American history. I have been asked what relevance Nonviolent Communication (NVC) has in such situations; what is the NVC response? I would say that one of the powerful aspects of NVC is that it invites all voices and listens to them. To illustrate:

An amazing thing happened in South Africa on February 14, 2018: Jacob Zuma resigned as president. He was forced from power for corruption without a single shot being fired. He was only the third president of South Africa since apartheid ended in 1991. How did such a young democracy pull off such a feat? I believe this amazing turn of events holds much relevance for us today in the U.S.A.

In 1996 when Nelson Mandela oversaw the enactment of a new democratic constitution for South Africa, he invited all political parties to participate, even those that got less than 2% of the vote. With everyone at the table, not only were all voices heard, but everyone went through the government-forming process and was exposed to the various issues and viewpoints. Thus, all parties had buy-in, and ratification went rather smoothly. I am convinced this inclusion was critical in forming a stable government and avoiding much carnage and death during the transition period.

Mandela's inclusive process was coupled with the truth and reconciliation process shepherded by Reverend Desmond Tutu. Truth and reconciliation has a lot in common with NVC. The atrocities and brutality of apartheid were aired openly and honestly (observations in NVC terms). The grief, anger, anguish, and remorse were welcomed (listening to feelings). Finally, the people who committed destructive acts met the people harmed by them. This human contact tended to dissolve rationalizations, stereotypes, justifications, and blame. Instead people saw other human beings and got glimpses into the situations and turmoil they were caught in (connecting with the universality of needs). This evoked empathy, and the desire for revenge and the perpetuation of violence diminished. There is still much violence and turmoil in South Africa, but they avoided a bloodbath when apartheid fell, and 27 years later they were able to force a corrupt president from power without firing a shot.

When all voices are invited and heard, stability flourishes. When voices are suppressed or shut out, strife ensues. Our society currently struggles with many voices vying for our attention, often trying to drown out all other voices. Our fraught political discourse with its evasive accusatory communication techniques, our inability to acknowledge error, our perception of compromise as weakness, all conspire to foment turmoil, vilification, and callous disregard.

While recently watching news footage from the 1950s and 1960s, I was struck by how much the current political discourse mirrors what was being said then. Many of the same arguments — about freedom to choose who your business serves, who you can rent to, the role of the Federal Government, and the rights of states — go back to the founding of this country and were central to our Civil War. As the writer Shelby Foote states at the beginning of Ken Burns' historic documentary, *The Civil War*, "Any understanding of this nation has to be based, and I mean firmly based, on an understanding of the Civil War. I believe this firmly. It defined us."

In my opinion, we have not healed from the Civil War, nor have we come to terms with the decimation visited upon the people and cultures that lived on this continent before Europeans arrived. These wounds continue to fester and drive our politics. I yearn for a comprehensive truth and reconciliation process around the role slavery and genocide played in forming this nation. I believe this would relieve us of a great burden. Below is an example of how this could look in modern times.

Currently, there is much rancor surrounding the removal of Confederate Civil War monuments. Many view them with trepidation as symbols of oppression and fear, while others hold them dear as indispensable parts of their cultural identity and heritage. I find truth in both perspectives. In the spirit of Nelson Mandela inviting all voices to the table, I advocate leaving the monuments standing, honoring bravery and sacrifice, yet augmenting them with memorials to the suffering that enslaved people endured or plaques commemorating the lives extinguished by lynching. The history is then more complete with many voices contributing to the discussion.

Our current "winner take all" form of politics — where opposing viewpoints are shouted down — is a recipe for violence and strife. I have witnessed this in both liberal and conservative contexts. The situation at our border grows out of a dysfunctional immigration policy that our leaders have been unable to address for decades. Even having reasonable discussion with members of the opposing side is cause for being voted out of office.

The power in the truth and reconciliation process is that it shifts our perception of the other side from enemy to fellow human. This does not automatically evaporate difference, nor should it. What it does is invite everyone to the table where solutions are forged. It requires us to embrace rather than flee from grief and remorse. We give up our allegiance to being right no matter what, and we can no longer pretend that we are the "superior enlightened one." However, in return we gain peace, security, and freedom.

Blame, vilification, and justification are easy, but reconciliation … reconciliation is not for the squeamish.

The Nitty-Gritty

On March 2, 2017, a student group at Middlebury College in Vermont invited Dr. Charles Murray — a luminary of the conservative movement — to speak about his new book. Knowing this would be controversial, they asked liberal-leaning Professor Allison Stanger to interview Murray after he spoke. Stanger was a well-liked and highly respected member of the faculty.

During the event, Murray was shouted down by protesting students. Adjourning to a private room with Stanger, they continued the interview, streaming it live over the internet and taking student questions via Twitter. At the end, as they stepped outside to leave, they were surrounded by protesters who knocked over 70-year-old Murray. When Stanger stepped in to help him, she was body-slammed. They finally got away, but Stanger ended up with a concussion that took several months to heal and was severe enough to prevent her from working.

In an October 10, 2017, interview on C-SPAN's Q&A, she recounted her experience to host Brian Lamb. At the conclusion of the interview she stated:

"Shutting down speech is an invitation to violence. We have these heated, passionate exchanges of view precisely to avoid having to pull out guns or swords or have a duel. So, when you shut down speech, you're basically inviting violence."

I tune into C-SPAN from time to time and watch House or Senate proceedings. I can only stomach so much. I grow weary of the endless stream of words, words, words. Then I remind myself that I much prefer words, words, words to bullets, bullets, bullets: something to think about the next time you hear someone expressing a view that upsets you.

If someone's words or beliefs arouse deep anger or fear in us, it helps to remember that anger and fear are physiological reactions to danger. They are designed to put our bodies on full alert, ready to spring into action to protect us. Our thinking brain shuts down so we are not distracted by analysis and can thus act rapidly, out of instinct. When we are jousting with words and there is no imminent physical danger, this physiological response is counter-productive and can actually increase the likelihood that violence will erupt.

There is something urgently important to us when anger and fear are aroused. Rather than going into instinctual fight, flight, freeze, we can use the steps below to defuse the situation.

1. Shift Our Focus From What We Are Against To What We Hold Dear: When we focus on what we value, what we stand for, rather than simply railing against what we object to or are threatened by, we set aside helplessness in favor of security, oppression in favor of innovation. We step into our power. From this empowered state, it is possible to creatively engage what we find threatening, building transformative connection and moving from conflict to common purpose. Honoring our deepest values awakens the wisdom in authenticity and invites us to trust in what matters most to us and draw strength from conviction.

2. Remember, Connecting Is More Powerful Than Convincing: Grounded in what we hold dear, in our own authenticity, our nervous system calms down, and we are able to listen rather than refute. We can become curious about views and actions that disturb us and seek to understand the motivations that support those positions. When we try to convince, it is easy for the person we are interacting with to tune us out. When we show that we are genuinely curious about what someone else holds dear, they are likely to care about what we hold dear. When we connect, it provides a foundation to begin seeking what we have in common rather than amplifying our differences.

3. Seek Common Ground: I was having a conversation with a conservative colleague. A vehement supporter of gun rights, he had a deep distrust of government. He told me that both George W. Bush and Barack Obama should be tried for treason and spend the rest of their lives in jail because they violated the U.S. Constitution. I was taken aback but became curious. I asked him how he came to that conclusion. We ended up having a lengthy and lively conversation about self-responsibility and freedom, and how freedom is at risk when we become complacent — something about which we both fervently agreed. Amid our authentic connection, his original assertion lost relevance. The last time I saw him, he flashed me a big smile and said, "David, I really enjoy talking with you. It makes me think!"

4. Practice: Ask yourself what is important to you, what are the bedrock values that guide your actions? Investigate. Why are they important? How do they serve you? Is your behavior consistent with these values? Are there even deeper underlying values? Make this a regular practice; it will bring the principles you value most to the forefront of your awareness. Then, when you hear something that upsets you, ask yourself what core value is threatened? Focus on that value. Remind yourself why it is so important to you. Invite its energy into your body; exude it. Now become curious about the interaction that upset you and respond in the spirit of your value. Invite your response itself to become an emissary of the value you treasure.

These are skills that must be cultivated through repetition and practice. It requires courage and perseverance. The rewards are authentic presence without posturing, meaningful connection without accommodation. This is the view from the trenches, the nitty-gritty work that forges solutions, diminishes violence, and spreads love.

What have you got to lose? Give it a try.

The detailed meditation at the end of this book walks you through this process.

We Welcome All

"We welcome all except those who don't welcome all."

Spring 2018: I was reminded of this saying last week while reading an article about detention conditions at the U.S.-Mexico border. At the bottom of the webpage was a box that began "Hate racists? Then read this … ." It was a come-on to induce you to subscribe to their daily news feed. "This site is not for me," I thought.

I can get angry, even livid, about the situation at the border, but is seems to me that hatred is the coin racists trade in. Hatred begets violence. From my point of view, labels such as liberal, conservative, left, right, Republican, and Democrat are superficial compared to what lives in one's heart. Hatred can mask itself under any of these labels. Love can express itself through any of these labels.

There is a phenomenon called "motive attribution asymmetry," where two opposing groups both believe that their side is motivated by love while the other side is motivated by hate. That very perception means they have something in common: their misunderstanding of one other. To acknowledge that you have something in common with those you view as an enemy can be difficult. To admit that they, too, are motivated by love may feel like betrayal.

Acknowledging does not mean agreeing or surrendering what you hold dear. In fact, disagreement is healthy; it keeps us vigorous and innovative. Acknowledging someone's perspective does mean becoming curious about their motivation, about how the world looks from where they stand.

Vilifying perpetuates misery. Curiosity beckons to solutions.

A Formula for Perpetuating Misery

Considering the border situation:

- you might abhor border agents as racist monsters who enjoy inflicting suffering without any respect for the values that make this county great;

- you might detest immigrant advocates as naive softies who have no idea about how the real world works and don't even love their country enough to defend it.

A Formula for Beckoning Solutions

Considering the border situation:

- you might wonder what it's like for border agents earning a paycheck by serving a country they are devoted to, overwhelmed by a sea of migrants who come on and on, yet constrained by policies and resources dictated by people insulated from the situation's urgent reality;

- you might wonder what drives immigrant advocates, many of whom volunteer their time to work on behalf of people who come from distant countries, well-meaning yet seemingly oblivious to how critical controlling our own borders is to our security as a nation.

Arthur Brooks, who just stepped down as president of the American Enterprise Institute, a conservative Washington think tank, urges us not to be "used by the outrage industrial complex." In a July 4, 2019, interview on the PBS News Hour, he stated that about 93% of Americans do not like the current polarization in the U.S.. However, about 7% of the population is getting rich, powerful, and famous by telling us it is OK to hate. He said that in a democracy, leaders are followers. They see a parade underway and jump in front of it so they can lead. If we stopped reading the columnists, watching the news shows, and following people on social media who promote hate, then politicians, journalists, and academics would "fall in line real quick."

He just published a book titled *Love Your Enemy* about answering hatred with love. He acknowledges this is not easy. In fact, he says, "It's hard, and the hardest thing is to conquer oneself."

Brooks said he set out to write an institutional book about creating better politics and better culture but ended up writing a book about how each one of us can become a better person. He said he was heavily influenced by the Dalai Lama who asks: "Can you conquer yourself? Are you the master or the slave of your own feelings?"

"That's the real challenge," Brooks said.

Working with feelings and learning to use them as guides to liberation is core to the Compassionate Communication work that I advocate.

Feelings touch on the "compassionate" aspect. I would like to share another brief story that touches on the "communication" aspect.

In October 1986, U.S. President Ronald Reagan and Mikhail Gorbachev, leader of the U.S.S.R., met in Reykjavik, Iceland, to discuss nuclear arms reduction. No treaty emerged from the meeting and at the time it was considered a failure.

In 1990, Gorbachev met with George Shultz, Reagan's Secretary of State, at Stanford University. Shultz said to Gorbachev: "When you entered office and when I entered office, the Cold War could not have been colder and when we left office it was basically over. What do you think was the turning point?"

Without hesitation, Gorbachev replied, "Reykjavik." Shultz asked why, expecting the Russian to talk about "missiles and stuff like that." Instead, Gorbachev replied: "Because for the first time the two leaders really had a deep conversation about everything. We really exchanged views and not just about peripheral things, but about the central things, and that was what was important about Reykjavik."

When people communicate authentically, miracles can happen!

Men Also Must Speak Up

I feel truly grateful to live in a culture where men and women work in partnership. When I was a young man in restaurant work, I was surrounded by women, including restaurant owners. When I worked with credit unions much of the senior management staff, including the CEOs, were women. Currently, the compassion work I engage in is filled with women. I cannot imagine a life where men and women are segregated. In such a world I would be bereft of many rich friendships.

The Me Too movement touches me deeply. There is much trauma in male/female relationships. Several women who have come forward with great courage to share their traumatic experiences have said, "We can't do this alone; men also must speak up."

This is a vulnerable topic for me, and I approach it with some trepidation. I fear inadvertently stepping on some "land mine" and arousing great animosity and misunderstanding. This has happened to me before. Today I will relate a simple example.

In my mid-20s, I was a waiter at the Mercury Cafe in downtown Denver. During lunch on Wednesdays a folk singer was paid to come and serenade us. Her voice was beautiful, and I greatly enjoyed her song choices. Working Wednesdays was fun and rich, thanks to her skill and art.

After a year or so, in gratitude, I wrote out one of my poems by hand and presented it to her with my thanks.

Two years later she came up to me and said, "I want to apologize." I had no idea what she was talking about. She went on to explain that when I gave her the poem she thought I was trying to hit on her. "I was furious with you for months. Eventually I realized that is just who you are, and you were simply saying thanks with no strings attached."

I was stunned, totally oblivious to the impact my gesture had evoked. I simply never would have guessed that my actions could be perceived as a come-on. Yet, I had to wonder what experiences of hers had caused her to automatically and genuinely perceive my actions as having a sexual agenda. We seemed to be living in different universes.

With the Me Too movement, those universes are becoming more visible. I find it both relieving and nerve-wracking. I have never before lived in a time when I have been so surprised and amazed by the unexpected, so unsure about what is coming next, or so certain that it must be met with empathy and compassion.

Dinner

In my late 20s, I took a woman I was quite fond of to a fairly exotic and expensive Moroccan restaurant. We had a delightful evening. After the meal she asked me how much it cost. When I told her, she expressed surprise. She explained that another male friend of ours had taken her to the same restaurant a few months earlier and had implied that the meal was much more expensive than it actually was.

"I let him kiss me even though I didn't want to," she explained.

"Why?" I asked.

"I felt guilty," she said. "I didn't feel like I could say no."

I found this totally baffling, yet not surprising. Baffling because my friend was a very outspoken, independent woman; not surprising because I knew the expensive "night on the town" was a tactic men often used to get into a woman's pants.

A main goal of Compassionate Communication is to shift our relationships from a domination or submission dynamic to one of partnership: power with, instead of power over. Thus, when we ask someone to do something, it is genuinely a request: We are enlisting their voluntary participation. There is a sweet and joyful affirmation that emerges when we know someone is joining us because they choose to do so, rather than because they feel compelled to do so. We also hold a tender vulnerability, because our request might be met with a "no."

One of the core topics in a comprehensive Compassionate Communication training is learning to "hear the yes behind the no." When we can hear what the other person is honoring within themselves, what they are saying "yes" to when they give us a "no," we move the focus from ourselves and our fear of rejection to the other person and their integrity. I would rather hear an honest "no" than a half-hearted "yes" any day.

Over the years, however, I have come to realize that for many, summoning the courage to say no in response to a request is extremely difficult. We are so eager to please and so yearn to contribute to another's happiness. We want to feel needed, that our presence holds value. Will we be the source of someone's disappointment? We may also fear anger that our "no" stimulates. Will there be retribution?

The "saying no" dynamic is profoundly amplified when it comes to male/female interactions. When I was young, I thought it was unfair that men were generally expected to make the first move, risking emotional rejection. It did not occur to me that women have much more at stake than men in such situations. Will they wake up to a humiliating rant on social media and find themselves in the midst of a shaming hurricane? Are they risking their jobs or promotion chances with dire economic consequences? Does saying no risk a physically violent response leading to assault or rape?

I now understand that there is much more than a sense of guilt and perceived obligation to please a man at stake when a woman says no and why my independent female friend may have felt compelled to say yes to a kiss she didn't want.

Wanna Play

The first time I wrote a Me Too inspired essay, I experienced considerable trepidation. Yet I was inspired enough by the bravery of women who said the movement needed men's voices, that I was able to set aside my misgivings. In this essay I want to return to that topic of courage.

A few years ago, around 9:00 in the evening, I headed out the back door of my apartment. As I turned the corner into the parking lot, I almost collided with my upstairs neighbor. She jumped back and screamed. Then she clutched her chest, breathing hard, and said, "Thank God it's you! I'm so sorry!"

I had long been in the habit of walking women to their cars at night and waiting until I saw them enter their front doors when I gave them a ride home. It was the encounter with my upstairs neighbor, however, when the different worlds men and women live in became real. Until then it had been an abstract concept that lived in my thought but not in my body.

The first thing that struck me about the incident with my neighbor was how embedded fright was in her nervous system. "What trauma had she endured to place it there?" I wondered. The second thing that struck me was that she immediately apologized for her fright as if she had done something wrong.

My news-following experience tells me that it is common for a woman to be criticized for not reporting an assault immediately. I have heard this used as a reason to deny the validity of their experience or to dismiss its intensity. When we experience trauma, it is a physiological phenomenon that lodges in our nervous system. We often want to become small, unnoticed, or to run away and hide. This drive is as irresistible as the compulsion to throw up when we have food poisoning or the instinct to avoid walking on a sprained ankle. I am deeply moved when women summon the courage to come forward about abuse.

In 1962 when I was 6, my family moved into Park Hill, a racially and economically integrated Denver neighborhood where I lived until I was 18. One summer day at age 11, I walked onto my front lawn and saw the boy who lived across the street a few doors down. He was around 14; even though we knew each other we did not hang out together much.

"Wanna play?" he inquired. "Sure," I answered. We headed toward his house. He reached into his pocket. "Like my new BB gun?" he asked. He then pointed the BB gun at me and said, "You had better do everything I say."

He took me to a vacant lot and told me to lie down in a shallow pit. He then started to place boards and dirt on me. "Are you going to bury me?" I asked, my voice quivering, barely holding tears at bay. He paused for a minute. "Get up," he said. We walked back to our street. He then pointed the gun at me again and said, "You better run," and boy did I! I had never moved so fast. As I sped down the street, he began shooting at me. One of the BBs hit the back of my neck. The welt took many months to subside.

I spent the rest of that day in a dream-like state. The world seemed distant and remote, the apparent calm not to be trusted. My 11-year-old mind grappled with the question, "What is real and what is an illusion?" I did not tell anyone about the incident. I wanted to be small and invisible, unnoticed. That seemed safest. I did not believe adults would understand, nor did I think they could protect me. After all, they could not protect me on the school playground where I was called names and my things were stolen; where I was told I better hide after school, and I was often laughed at. The run-in with the boy with the BB gun was not unfamiliar: a bit more intense and frightening, but of similar spirit.

Compared to many of the Me Too stories that have come out, my encounter was mild. So, I can well imagine how easy it would be after severe trauma to mistrust your perception of reality, or want to disappear and not be noticed, or to question if you are the one who did something wrong. I also appreciate how difficult it is to speak out if you don't think people will take you seriously or protect you from further harm. This has to be particularly difficult if the abuse involves, as it often does, someone you see or interact with on a regular basis, especially if they have authority over your livelihood or are part of your family configuration.

I don't remember ever again crossing paths with the boy with the BB gun. I don't think he was particularly vicious or "bad." I think he had a new toy, and he wanted to use it. I think he was so focused on his BB gun that he didn't really notice that I was a person as he ordered me around. When I asked him if he was going to bury me, I think he sort of woke up and realized his actions were having an impact on me.

I hope the Me Too movement helps us see one another as flesh-and-blood human beings. I think much of the behavior exposed by Me Too is thoughtless habit that may seem acceptable because it is so common. When we see that other flesh-and-blood human, kinship awakens and we can't help but notice the impact our actions have. Our behavior becomes deliberate and conscious.

Bringing behavior into conscious awareness often exposes trauma. Trauma is not the exclusive domain of women. Witness the revelations about abuse of boys currently rocking our religious and civic communities.

Over the last two decades men who had remained silent about their horrific World War II experiences finally began speaking out, much to their own benefit and that of their families. It was hailed as a major cultural event. I saw many a tear-filled and joyful documentary as these men released burdens they had been carrying for decades. Viewers were both moved and inspired by their stories.

The shedding of this stoic pretense and silence was unthinkable before the Vietnam War. During Vietnam images showing the brutality of war were, for the first time, broadcast into our living rooms. Some Vietnam veterans began speaking out about their experiences and the issues they faced when they returned. Many young men questioned the war itself and refused to serve, risking jail or fleeing to Canada. During this era of "America, love it or leave it," speaking out and questioning authority was considered unpatriotic. It was the wake of the "red scare," the House Un-American Activities Committee, and the Hollywood blacklist. The pressure to remain silent was immense. People put their livelihoods and sometimes their lives on the line because the truth that burned in them could not be kept silent.

Similarly, the courage I see in women breaking their silence and speaking out today burns brightly in my soul, nourishing me with inspiration and determination. Me Too expresses a universal human yearning, an insistence that we all be treated with respect. It demonstrates the courage that emerges when we realize we are not alone. When we speak out and our cries fall on deaf ears, we cower in shame, weighed down by guilt. We wonder if we truly matter and begin to doubt our own existence, our own perception of reality. Me Too is powerful because it acknowledges our cries and validates the wounding we feel. It brings light and warmth to darkness; we become visible and unfrozen.

A Cub Scout Parade

In honor of Holocaust Remembrance Day on January 27, 2018, I heard an interview on CPR Colorado Matters with Denver Holocaust survivor Jack Adler. He said something that deeply resonated with my commitment to spreading compassionate consciousness:

"I'm very proud of my Jewish heritage, however, I'm not what you would consider very religious. What I believe is that God created man, and man created evil. We are responsible for how we treat or mistreat each other."

"We don't have to love everyone. We don't even have to like everyone, but we should respect everyone because mutual respect and the golden rule 'do unto others as you like them to do unto you' is the key to the survival of humanity. Until humanity, in my opinion, embraces this we will continue to destroy each other."

It reminded me of something similar that psychologist Marshall Rosenberg, who developed Nonviolent Communication (NVC), said:

"Our survival as a species depends on our ability to recognize that our well-being and the well-being of others are in fact one and the same."

When we rush to judgment, demonize one another, and treat people as stereotypes and caricatures rather than thinking, feeling human beings, we perpetuate violence and suffering. There is an assumption that understanding where someone is coming from implies that you agree with them, that even taking the time to sincerely listen is a betrayal of your own values. This assumption is one of the largest impediments to peace that we face. It is also the one most easily dispelled by empathy.

NVC and Compassionate Communication instill self-confidence and inner security so that we are not threatened by views different from our own. It gives us the strength and courage to listen sincerely and embrace that golden rule Jack Adler refers to. It is the way of empathy.

Here is an amazing example of these principles put into action.

Amid our social turbulence, I have been asked, "How would you approach the Ku Klux Klan?" Daryl Davis, a black musician, has been doing that for the past 30 years. Davis has become friends with many Klansmen, some of whom renounced their Klan ties after getting to know him.

As a child, Davis marched in a Cub Scout parade and was pummeled with rocks and bottles by people standing along the parade route just because he was black. The question, "How can you hate me when you don't even know me?" became the focus of much of his young life. At age 10, he began reading books on racism and white supremacy. By the time he was an adult, after reading thousands of pages in numerous books, he still did not have an answer to that question, so he decided to ask racists directly. Thus, began his multi-decade exploration, as a black man, into the KKK.

In an October 25, 2017, interview on C-SPAN's Q&A, he explained: "Ignorance breeds fear. If you don't keep that fear in check, that fear will breed hatred because we hate those things that frighten us. If you don't keep that hatred in check, it will breed destruction."

He went on to explain that many of the Klan members he met were ignorant: "You have people who are ignorant and you have people who are stupid and, you know, we all are ignorant to a certain degree because we don't know everything, but an ignorant person is someone who can learn."

When they got to know Davis as a thinking, feeling human being they learned that the stereotypes and caricatures of black people that their ignorance enabled were simply inaccurate, and they were changed. Many of them reevaluated their relationship with the Klan and renounced it. This did not work with everyone, Davis noted.

When asked how he gets Klansmen to see him as a human being, he said, "I listen to them and genuinely try to understand where they are coming from."

He expressed gratitude for the election of President Trump because "People are openly talking about racism, when before they swept it under the rug and pretended we had resolved it."

"I have been living with racism for 30 years," he added, "but people are going about it the wrong way to resolve it. People are talking about each other, or they're talking at each other. I sit down to talk with each other. I never set out to convert anyone. I set out to listen."

Davis' story is a testimonial to the power of Compassionate Communication if ever there was one. Our times yearn for compassionate responses. Daryl Davis provides a powerful example to emulate.

Perceptual Bubbles

Our sanity demands continuity. When we don't trust our perception, we are beset with insecurity, anxiety, and confusion. In my opinion, our society is experiencing trauma due to a lack of shared reality. We live in perceptual bubbles reinforced by Facebook, by Twitter, by where we consume our news, and by the like-minded people we surround ourselves with. When these reality bubbles collide, it can be traumatic and feel like our survival is in question. Our nervous systems mobilize for protection, and we find ourselves in conflict.

I heard an interview with a student survivor of the April 20, 1999, mass shooting at Colorado's Columbine High School. He described the helplessness he felt huddled in a classroom, knowing that if a shooter came through the door there was nothing anyone could do to defend themselves: They were sitting ducks. He now strongly supports arming teachers.

Soon after the Marjory Stoneman Douglas High School mass shooting on February 14, 2018, Florida's Senator Marco Rubio held a town hall meeting, knowing he would be facing an angry and hostile crowd. One of the student survivors said, "When I look at you, I see a mass murderer." This student strongly supports a ban on the public sale of assault weapons.

Two realities in collision. Two nervous systems mobilized for protection, insistent on asserting their validity. Two perceptual bubbles in conflict, breeding insecurity. Two traumatized people. A society in turmoil. How do we coax trauma out of the cold darkness and welcome it into the warm light where it can unwind and free us from its compulsive dictates? How do we cultivate a shared reality with continuity and stability where people feel secure, seen, and acknowledged?

From the Compassionate, Nonviolent Communication perspective, we start by listening. We start by getting in touch with the helplessness and terror the former Columbine student felt, weaponless with gun-wielding madmen on the other side of a locked door. We start by acknowledging the rage of the Stoneman Douglas student, reeling from the deaths that suddenly and unexpectedly swooped into his life, outraged that someone with the shooter's troubled history could walk into a store and buy a military weapon with about as much effort as it takes to get a library card.

By letting both students know we understand their feelings, acknowledging the intensity of the situations, and honoring what they hold important, we bring to awareness the intensity and sincerity they hold in common: We begin to interact with people, not ideologies. We get a glimpse into perceptual bubbles and begin building a shared reality. This calms the nervous system, and we can move from a fight, flight, freeze defensive posture into creative engagement where the entire brain is activated and attentive, where insight and inspiration aid our problem-solving genius. This is difficult work and requires courage, dedication, and persistence, but it spawns pragmatic results and averts bloodshed.

This is the view from the Compassionate Nonviolent Communication perceptual bubble

Violence And Antibodies

"Sticks and stones can break my bones, but words, words can inspire someone to pick up those sticks and stones."

Psychologist Marshall Rosenberg, Ph.D., started developing Nonviolent Communication (NVC) in the 1960s out of his desire to find ways for humans to interact that support one another rather than contend with one another. He pioneered a linguistic technology that draws us into deep connection with ourselves while resonating with the humanity in others. The resulting desire to contribute to one another's well-being transforms violent desperation into constructive innovation.

We are in the midst of great turbulence, both nationally and globally, amplified by our technological potency. Weapons are more deadly than ever while social media spreads ideologies at an unprecedented pace. Nonviolent Communication also emerged from this technological potency: We understand our biology, neurology, and psychology at a depth undreamed of some 100 years ago when Freudian theory was all the rage. It is easy for me to view NVC as arising just so we would have the tools to effectively respond to our discordant times.

According to Wikipedia, in the U.S. "As of August 4, 2019, 251 mass shootings have occurred in 2019 .... This averages out to 1.2 shootings per day. In these shootings, 979 people were shot; of those people, 246 have died."

The motives ascribed are many: personal vendettas, allegiance to Islamic groups, defending the white race from invasion, standing up to right-wing fascism, turf wars, and criminal intimidation, while some motives are simply incoherent.

Hatred and fanaticism can express through any ideology or rationale, any culture or ethnicity. So can love and moderation. A common thread weaving through the backgrounds of many of these shooters is a feeling of isolation, of not mattering. Extremist hate groups can provide a sense of purpose and kinship that captivates and welcomes; it can provide direction and meaning. Those who feel discarded and ignored can find respect and acceptance. They become devotees, and many express that devotion through violence.

In general, much of our current political upheaval arises from frustrated people feeling invisible and ignored. Their needs are not addressed by the political system, their voices are not included in the public discourse, their financial plight is not acknowledged in economic reporting, and their concerns are simply not understood.

Inclusion and visibility are essential to a stable society. They ease the intensity and isolation that fuel hatred and violence. NVC is an incredibly effective tool for cultivating inclusion and shared purpose. Often, we are profoundly unaware of how our actions appear to others simply because we lack the experiential context that sculpts their perception. Making visible these experiential differences reduces tension, awakens shared purpose, and enables us to remain in deep connection with ourselves while resonating with the humanity in others.

There is now much research showing that violence spreads in much the same way a viral epidemic spreads: transmitted from person to person, neighborhood to neighborhood, region to region. Based on this research, new forms of intervention to defuse gang violence are being pioneered, with an emphasis on proactive conversation and increased skills for processing feelings.

Building skills that endow each of us with authenticity, inspiration, and resolve — which serve as "antibodies" to stop the spread of violence — is central to why I devote myself to this work.

Self-Criticism

I was heavily picked on in school. Thus, during the September 27, 2018, U.S. Senate hearing with Christine Blasey Ford and Brett Kavanaugh, the attacking bravado exhibited by Kavanaugh was hauntingly familiar. Many, many people take comfort from such behavior. It symbolizes strength, courage, standing up for yourself. It also implies an enemy and a hostile world perpetually out to get you; a world where safety requires unending vigilance and aggression. It is a world where you can't relax. I would also venture that it is a world that bespeaks a fundamental mistrust of life and a deep insecurity.

Albert Einstein famously said, "The most fundamental question we can ever ask ourselves is whether or not the universe we live in is friendly or hostile."

I live in a friendly universe where I trust life. I haven't stopped breathing yet.

Even when I was miserable in junior high school — when classmates would steal my things, shove and trip me in the halls, or yell foul things at me after school — I knew there was no outside "rescuer" who could save me. Insecurity was the nemesis that plagued me. Transforming that insecurity and finding confidence became the main focus of my life. It took many years of determined effort to learn to trust myself and quiet the endless stream of self-criticism occupying my thoughts. Ultimately, I was the bully, criticizing myself far more than any classmate ever did. Convinced as I was of my own inadequacy, that constant stream of self-criticism was an attempt to guide me to safety, make me a better person, encourage my confidence. It did not work well.

That is exactly the dynamic I see playing out on the national and international stage: a ceaseless quest for security and stability that ever eludes, mired in perpetual uncertainty. In my case, learning to listen to my self-criticism and understanding what it wanted to accomplish were key to transforming it. I gave myself empathy, and it healed me. Empathy can also heal on a cultural level. Empathy from Jewish college friends transformed Derek Black, son of a grand wizard of the Ku Klux Klan, from one of the rising stars of the white nationalist movement to one of its most insightful critics. He wrote, with Eli Saslow, *Rising Out of Hatred*, a book that chronicles his transformation.

When I was in junior high school during the late 1960s, there were riots in several large cities. National leaders were assassinated, and thousands were dying each month in Vietnam. When the Pentagon Papers were leaked in March 1971, we discovered that our political leaders were not being truthful about the Vietnam War. Soon after came the Watergate scandal, forcing the resignation of President Richard Nixon in 1974. I grew up amid relentless criticism of our government. It has not abated to this day. Government as "the enemy" is a mainstay of political discourse. As a nation, we are caught in a cycle of self-criticism and low self-esteem. It is no wonder that bullying is rampant as we engage in that ceaseless search for a security and stability that ever eludes. Government is an expression of our collective consciousness. Just as I was ultimately the bully, criticizing myself, when we ceaselessly criticize government we criticize us. I should know. My time in high school when I most severely criticized myself is also the time I most severely criticized government. As I have made peace with myself, my admiration for government and the complexity it must navigate has grown.

It is no small accomplishment to have lights that turn on at the flip of a switch and grocery stores where I can effortlessly harvest dinner. Governments provide the underlying coherence that makes these conveniences possible. I have developed empathy for government. As far as I know, empathy is the only way to break the ceaseless cycle of criticism that distracts our society from the impending global challenges that threaten civilization. Empathy enables us to understand one another and unleash the collective creativity that built civilization in the first place.

My influence on government is distant and abstract. My influence on myself is up close and personal. As my self-trust grew and I began to listen to and understand my self-criticism rather than push it away, my confidence grew. As I became more confident, bullying behavior had less impact on me. I remember bumping into junior-high classmates years later only to discover that they remembered me with fondness, while I remembered them with fear.

A few years ago, I arranged a meeting with a potential solar energy client who brought along his business partner. The partner began telling me how incompetent I was, how I was wasting his time and that I better get my shit together. My old pattern would have been to cringe and apologize. Instead, I met his hostility with polite calm while thinking to myself, "His reaction obviously has nothing to do with me. I wonder why he is so angry?"

Self-empathy grew my confidence and self-esteem to a level where I can now remain calm and empowered in the midst of adversity and intensity. This has dramatically increased my ability to create fulfilling connections with a diverse variety of people and has opened my eyes to perspectives I never imagined.

Working with self-empathy is as local as it gets and yet the impact is global beyond comprehension.

Anxiety About Anxiety

Anxiety And Me

When I feel fear, I freeze. Sometimes, as I prepare to write an essay, I go through a day or two of anxiety where I can't type a single word. My eyes get heavy and begin to burn, and my stomach wants food even though I am not hungry. No matter how pleased I am with previous essays or how much people tell me they like them, this pattern persists. Over time I have become quite familiar with it; I have even learned to befriend it.

This has proven a welcome transformation. I used to feel anxiety about my anxiety. After all, I had a deadline: I had to get something done! I needed to get off my butt and get busy! Meanwhile, I would lie there in immobilized torment for months at a time. What was wrong with me? After all, I knew better.

Anxiety about my anxiety, produced anxiety about my anxiety about my anxiety, which produced anxiety about my anxiety about my anxiety about my anx.......

Caught in this endless whirlpool, I felt trapped and broken, desperate for escape. My ability to get things done was diminished. I railed about self-sabotage and called myself an idiot. I studied self-help, philosophy, religion, and I went into therapy.

It worked.

I learned not to be afraid of my fear, not to get anxious about my anxiety. I did this by paying attention; by not trying to send it away, fix it, or distract myself. I just listened. Listening, I realized my fear indicated that what I was doing was important to me, that it mattered, that I wanted to do a good job and contribute value. I still have that fear, but it is no longer accompanied by fright and dismay. Now I accompany it with patience and understanding. It still impacts my ability to get things done, but the cycle runs for two hours or two days instead of two months and does not dominate my life the way it once did.

Anxiety And The World

Learning to work with fear is a great calling of our time. In 2016 we went through a presidential election with extraordinarily high turnout and several razor-thin margins of victory where fear was front and center. I did not see the election as contention between Democrats and Republicans, rural and urban, left and right, conservative and liberal. I saw it as a choice: Do we want to live in a world guided by fear and hatred or a world guided by love and compassion?

Hatred can wear a liberal mask or a conservative mask.

Compassion can wear a conservative mask or a liberal mask.

A fear-laced world: In a fear-laced world there are winners and losers, someone must be right and someone must be wrong, and if you are wrong you must be punished. In a fear-laced world one person's gain is another person's loss, and the loser deserves it. In a fear-laced world you had better protect yourself because enemies lurk everywhere. In a fear-laced world you better not trust anyone, and you better make sure events go the way you want. It is a world of opportunists, so buyers better beware. It is a world where letter bombs arrive in the mail, where the best defense is a strong offense, survival training is a must. It is a world where you are constantly scanning your environment, on the look-out for pitfalls and predators. This is a world rife with violence. It is also a world of the endless adrenaline rush and the noble cause that must be championed. It is a compelling world that tests one's cunning, courage and resourcefulness.

A love-saturated world: In a love-saturated world, neighbors show up to help when natural disasters strike, communities creatively coalesce to solve problems, resources are abundant and shared, collaboration is exhilarating, and one person's gain is another person's gain. In a love-saturated world we are seen and accepted for who we are, and trust is repaid with meaning. In a love-saturated world we feel secure and inspired, we know our presence matters. It is a world where the big challenges are: "How fully can I express myself? How big do I dare dream? How much bliss can I stand?" It is a world of deep peace and wonder where individual sovereignty and communal responsibility naturally balance. It is a world of the endlessly miraculous.

Anxiety And Empathy

As a nation today, we seem caught in an irresistible whirlpool of blame and recrimination. I find it strikingly similar to the storms that used to rage in my head. Much of our political engagement is dominated by fear, and many people feel frightened by how prominent a role fear plays. I am one of them. There is also a great deal of anxiety and worry in society right now. There are people who feel anxious about the level of anxiety and want desperately to soothe it. Just as fear and anxiety used to paralyze me, our political leaders seem immobilized by partisan torment.

I am not immune from this turmoil. I am not consumed by it either. My earlier inner work with fear and anxiety serves as an inculcation so I can listen to the political rancor with patience and understanding. By listening instead of banishing, I learned not to be afraid of my fear, not to get anxious about my anxiety.

The same dynamic applies as I listen to world news and political posturing. When I encounter vehement, angry debate and recrimination, I listen for what is important, for what matters to the participants that arouses such passion. I may still disagree with what is said, feeling fear or anger, but I am not consumed by panic and dismay or an urge to convince and discredit.

When I listen intently, I don't perceive a posture or a position or a sinister special-interest group or a misguided, ignorant, uninformed, brainwashed idiot. I perceive a flesh-and-blood human being with a beating heart and questing brain expressing something of vital importance to them as they grapple with a complex, rapidly changing world.

Beware! This approach is likely to sprout friendship amid animosity and cause you to be less certain you are right. In fact, you may discover there is nothing to argue about at all.

What I am describing is empathy, the urgent calling of our times, the salve that can heal a wounded world, the porthole that leads from the world of fear and hatred into the world of love and compassion.

Getting with the times, I see that bluster is in vogue these days. Who am I to resist popular trends? So here goes:

Those who grasp for power using the blame-and-vilify strategy often express disdain and contempt for empathy as weak and impotent. They are wise to be suspect. Empathy is the biggest threat to blame-and-vilify tactics. Empathy renders them ineffective. Stuff that under your hat and stew on it!

Part Three

Empathy

The heart opens:

The mind expands,
Insight erupts,
Inspiration ignites,
Consciousness blooms;

Pain succumbs to bliss,
Grief becomes a sacrament,
Peace resides in gratitude,
Compassion illuminates action;

Desires find spontaneous fulfillment,
Life dances effortlessly and endlessly,
All is present, all is miraculous,
And play abounds!

Turning Away

My father died a few months before I entered first grade. The first day at school, standing with a group of classmates, I blurted out, "Guess what? I don't have a dad."

As I said this, the kids who had been looking at me turned away and began talking among themselves as if they could not hear me. It seemed I did not exist. I remember feeling incredibly stupid and invisible. In that moment, my perception become flat and dream-like. It was as if I were watching events on a movie screen but was not part of the picture. I became withdrawn and distant; many, many years passed before I again dared to share what was important to me. My isolation felt safe but lonely. Yet, that feeling of safety was itself a sham. I dreaded being discovered as some unworthy impostor, unfit for friendship or even attention. I became distant from myself in an attempt to hold anxiety and insecurity at bay, afraid that I would drown in it.

Decades later (after some really good therapy and world-class workshops), I realized that I had been treating my anxiety and insecurity in the exact same way my first-grade classmates had treated me: Pretending I did not hear, pretending it did not exist. Invisible.

Discomfort — profound discomfort — impelled me to turn away from myself, protecting me from feelings I did not yet know how to handle. As this insight emerged, I also realized that my first-grade classmates probably felt a similar discomfort when I spoke about my dad, and it impelled them to look away. They were not out to shun me; they were protecting themselves.

This realization lifted a great burden from my life. Being able to welcome my anxiety and insecurity soothed my loneliness, and thus my anxiety and insecurity diminished. Now I am able to talk candidly with people about traumatic events, to their great relief.

We often see one another, or ourselves, through a prism. We focus on what should be, filtering out and hiding from our perceived unworthiness. This denial leaves pretense in its wake and is a formula for loneliness and isolation. When we accept one another or ourselves as we are right now, relaxation emerges, and liberation ensues.

We call this empathy.

Empathy helps us understand and recognize ourselves. Revealing what we truly care about, it brings us into resonance with our dearest values. Empathy helps us see others as they see themselves. What matters to each of us becomes visible, and we experience authenticity and accompaniment while pretense and loneliness fade.

Running from my loneliness, I was trapped by it because it controlled my actions. Alone, I could not digest my loneliness; I needed others. I needed accompaniment. Absolutely critical to ending my isolation was being around people who accepted me as I was. This unconditional acceptance helped me accept myself. My lack of self-acceptance, after all, was the source of my loneliness and isolation.

Conscripted child soldiers returning to their villages in Africa are largely able to heal from the scars of war when their communities accept them and welcome their return.

Where the villagers shun and blame them, post-traumatic stress and psychotic reactions are common.

Empathy? Invisibility? Which world do you want to live in?

Keep the Music Playing

Marshall Rosenberg, the psychologist who developed Nonviolent Communication, talked about "natural giving," which is how we find meaning and fulfillment through contribution. A few years ago, I was listening to Tony Bennett and Aretha Franklin singing the Alan and Marilyn Bergman song, "How Do You Keep the Music Playing?" One of the phrases from the song stuck with me:

> *How do you lose yourself*
> *To someone*
> *And never lose your way?*

Have you ever gotten into a relationship where you wanted to help someone and found yourself thinking, "I've got to get them to understand ... . If only they would ... . Can't they see how wonderful they ... ." Before long you can totally lose touch with your own self and your needs, suppressing what is important to you in order to serve them.

Have you ever hidden yourself in order to protect someone else from "the truth," or to fit in to what you think they expect so you will be accepted, or because it is just plain scary to let someone know what you truly care about? Have you become so defined by what you think the other person needs that you "forget" who you are and feel empty, depleted, or incomplete?

I suspect these experiences are common. I know I sure have had them, as have many of my friends. How do we keep the music playing in a relationship? How do we keep it fresh and alive? How do we interact with the present rather than playing out scripted past patterns?

I have long pondered the balance between autonomy and community. I believe the more connected we are with ourselves, the more connected we can be with others. When relationships become an exploration rather than a burden, when they are partnerships rather than power struggles, then they hold deep meaning and intimate connection.

Setting boundaries and expressing authentically: These are the skills that support autonomy and enable our actions to be grounded in choice and freedom. Then we can deeply accompany those we love and be responsive to their needs without having to suppress our own.

Be bold and ask for what is important to you! Be audacious enough to not "go along" when your heart says "No!" Take a risk and trust that someone will welcome your authenticity! Dare to journey together in partnership with those you care for! Awaken the courage to live in vulnerability and find meaning!

This is one way to keep the music playing and lose yourself in another without losing your way.

A Thousand Miles

We have all heard that a journey of a thousand miles begins with a single step. I would add that you must start from where you are. When you get directions from Google Maps or MapQuest, you must enter your point of departure as well as your destination. If you don't know where you are to begin with, the directions won't work no matter how detailed.

Knowing your starting point: That is why authenticity is so essential and so empowering. No matter how brilliant and powerful the teaching or wisdom tradition, if we are adrift in confusion and denial, hiding from ourselves, afraid to practice honesty, we will flounder amid helplessness because we are unclear about our starting point. The directions, no matter how clever and profound, simply will not be able to guide us to our destination. "Know thyself" is one of the oldest and most fundamental of empowerment teachings. It can also be one of the most difficult.

We often feel confusion and ambiguity because we are protecting ourselves from inner pain and wounding or a fear that we are inadequate. Sometimes we are motivated to protect those we love by hiding from them some truth we deem hurtful. All of these are reasons we struggle with authenticity. Compassion provides a warm accompaniment that fortifies and nourishes us as we struggle. Compassionate self-acceptance ferments authenticity and summons courage.

Redressing pain, cleansing wounds, expressing spontaneously and freely, finding the courage to trust those we love: These are the fruits of a compassionate practice. Those called to such a practice begin that thousand-mile journey with a firm, resolute, and productive step.

Support

An enduring house is supported by a well-laid foundation. A well-designed chair supports your back. I sometimes hear on the news that consumer spending supports our economy. Political figures are supported by their base. When we want help undertaking a project, we ask for support. People join support groups to help them through times of difficulty.

In fact, without support our capabilities are severely limited. Lacking support, we can feel alone, overwhelmed, and uncertain. Just as a building's foundation depends on stable bedrock, our security depends on a coherent and stable reality. When we look to ever-shifting and turbulent circumstances for that stability, it is akin to laying a foundation in sand, and our well-being seems dubious. We become plagued by doubt and insecurity. This is driving much of the social turmoil we currently experience.

Consistent across all of our experiences is that we are there. Our own presence is the one thing we can depend on.

How do we show up? How do we welcome that presence? What about our presence supports us and attends to our well-being? Since we bring ourselves to our every experience, what within us can we depend on for consistency and security?

Presence is our emissary into reality, our direct connection to life. Embracing our presence is embracing life: endlessly innovative, resilient, and consistent. Knowing yourself, self-connection, is the underlying bedrock that supports our reality. It puts us in direct contact with the force that animates our being, draws our breath, and beats our heart.

Knowing that who we are right now in this moment is enough and that we need be nothing other than who we are is the Great Work. We wrestle with doubt, encounter shame, spar with guilt, play hide-and-seek with suppressed parts of ourselves, and endure endless self-criticism. Yet all the while we are searching for the loving intention behind our actions and struggling to accept ourselves because we know that is what we are supposed to do if we want to be free.

In the past when I did or said something I regretted, I would to say to myself, "David, you idiot!" Now I say, "David, I love you!"

As my self-talk has shifted, so has the way I relate to others. Before, when people asked to talk with me, I entered the conversation apprehensive and closed, ready to defend myself or explain why they were wrong. Now, I become still and ready to listen. Often I find myself saying, "Thank you, I had no idea I came across that way," or "I am so glad we talked, because what I intended is so different from what you perceived."

Recently a friend said to me, "You ask me to do something and after I've done it you explain how you would have done it differently and why yours was the better way to do it." Boy, was I grateful! Familiar with this unconscious pattern, I thought I had expunged it from my life. Discovering it was still active was a great service, especially since my friend brought it up right as it was happening. I responded to her, "Thank you for telling me. Whenever I do that, please let me know right away. It really helps me bring it into consciousness so I can change it."

In that moment I felt deeply supported.

Another recent conversation involved someone who helps out when I conduct trainings. He was showing reluctance to continue and asked if we could talk. He recounted a time when we were packing up after a class. I told him I could improvise during lessons because I had been doing this kind of work for over 30 years, whereas someone just starting out finds that following the lesson plan closely provides an invaluable support. What he heard in my comment was, "I am way better at this than you are, and I don't want to work with you anymore." What I thought I was conveying was, "Getting good at this takes lots of practice. There is no substitute for experience. You are just starting out so persevere and practice, and your skill will grow." I consider this person a real trooper dedicated to Nonviolent Communication and thought I was encouraging him. Again, another conversation I am grateful for!

The change in my relationship to "the talk" — from apprehension to gratitude — is not something I "figured out." Rather, when my relationship with myself shifted from criticism to acceptance, my relationship to others shifted automatically. I can't explain how; it just happened.

Ultimately, affirming the I Am, accepting and welcoming ourselves while treating ourselves with love and kindness leads to a security and confidence that is unperturbed by ever-shifting and turbulent circumstances. It is precisely because we look to love, acceptance, welcome, and kindness for support that we are consistently supported by love, acceptance, welcome, and kindness.

Beyond the reach of time, they are consistent, unchanging, eternal, and ever present.

Atlas

When I was 20 or so, my church was interviewing for a new minister. One candidate met with the high-school youth group, where I was an adviser. The U.S. had just gotten out of Vietnam, Richard Nixon had resigned, the women's liberation movement was gaining full steam, and anti-nuke demonstrations were rampant.

I asked our prospective minister what he thought the world needed to solve our problems. He responded that he did not have the wisdom to answer that question. At the time I considered this answer a cop-out. My mind was full of sentences like: "What we need to do is … ." and "If only people would … ." and "It's obvious that these problems are caused by … ."

Arrogance, idealism, or naivety? I was sincere in my desire to alleviate suffering and quick to judge that with which I disagreed. It took me another 30 years to honestly admit that I did not have all the answers. During those decades I would pretend humility, sometimes fooling even myself. But it was not until I truly surrendered attachment to outcome that I realized people with whom I disagreed were not simply unaware and misguided. Sometimes they actually had valid perspectives. In fact, there were times when I was the misguided one!

Uncomfortable as these realizations were, they also brought great liberation. I no longer had to carry the "weight of the world" on my shoulders. I only had to be responsible for myself (of course, that meant giving up my addictions to guilt and blame).

Atlas — the Greek god who carries the world on his shoulders — is imprisoned by his role, unable to seek rest or relief lest the world crumble. Believing oneself essential to the world's well-being is a form of arrogance that held me captive for decades, yet the desires fueling it were genuine and loving.

Only when we can see beauty instead of brokenness in others and we learn to trust them with their own destinies can we be fully free. Thinking "if only they would … ." or "what they should do is … ." or "how can they manage without my help?" holds us captive, unable to seek rest or relief lest the world crumble. It is when we surrender such thinking that we can step out from under the weight of the world and set down burdens that are not ours. Liberated, we can then love freely and unconditionally.

How do we set down such burdens? How do we release our attachments to outcome? It begins with trust. When we recognize that at our root we are all motivated by love and a strong desire to contribute, our urge to control diminishes. When we admit that we don't have all the answers and we don't know what to do in every situation, we can see that solutions emerge and others still care for themselves. Then we begin to relax, and trust naturally surfaces.

This process is often referred to as surrendering ego. I have heard it said that love dissolves ego. I don't think ego goes away. Ego is essential to maintaining our identity. My experience is that ego steps out of its role as Atlas and discovers itself part of a vast and wondrous world where it is not compelled to do anything in particular. Rather it gets to explore endless possibilities and choose the ones that joyfully fulfill its destiny. Now that's freedom!

I Hurt Therefore I Am

My credo used to be: "I hurt, therefore I am." I measured how much I loved someone by how much pain I was able to endure "on their behalf." I truly believed that by suffering in a relationship I was opening myself to love. At the same time, I went to great lengths to try and relieve the suffering from those I cared about. I was totally blind to this contradiction, and it created a huge tension in my life. No matter how desperately I wanted to alleviate suffering, I was dependent on it for love and meaning.

My devotion to pain and woundedness — in service to love — prevented me from accepting others as they were. I would automatically assume something needed to be fixed and dwell on who they could be if only they changed. My blindness to this dynamic also prevented me from accepting myself. No matter what, I was never "good enough." These were desperate and lonely times. The more I strived for love, the more pain I felt, and the lonelier I became.

I remember the moment, in my early 30s, when this began to change. At the time, I thought in terms of self-sabotage and failure mechanisms. I was at war with me, thinking I had to conquer my behavior, break through my blocks. Still, I was possessed of an earnest desire to transform and escape the prison "of my own making."

On a warm summer day, sitting on the living room couch, I started breathing deeply, inviting my body to relax and stilling my thoughts. I then connected with the "failure-prone, destructive" part of myself and imagined it shrinking as it receded down a long tunnel. I thought I was sending my subconscious the message that I did not want to act in self-destructive ways anymore.

The failure-prone part of me had nearly vanished down the tunnel when its departure suddenly accelerated as if it had received an extra energetic push. At the same time, a voice seemingly behind me said, "Yeah, get rid of that energy." In that instant, I realized the very energy I was trying to banish had "snuck around behind me" and was camouflaging as my own intention to banish it. I spontaneously burst out laughing. "Pretty sneaky," I said. My body felt light and agile, my mood playful and buoyant as if a weight had been lifted from my life as, in fact, it had.

Two life-changing insights arose immediately from that experience.

First the "sneaky" part of myself felt pretty cocky and arrogant. I realized that arrogance motivated my attempts to relieve suffering in others: "I know what's best for you … . If only you could see … ." Once I recognized this arrogance I could not "un-recognize" it, and I became much less sure that I knew what was best for others.

The second realization I had was that encoded in my helping attitude was the implication: "You are weak and helpless, not sturdy enough to handle life. I must protect you from yourself and from the truth because you can't be trusted with it."

All of this in the name of love.

Changing my habitual behavior and default perception took me many years, but it happened. When I finally give up my perception that people needed to be "fixed," my goal became connection simply for the fulfillment connection brings. I began trusting that connection, and I discovered that joy naturally arises from contributing freely with no strings attached. Suffering evaporated, replaced by sacrament.

One final realization awaited me, the one that firmly anchored my other insights: Under it all I was simply trying to take care of myself, to be safe, to belong, and to contribute. Even back in the "I hurt, therefore I am" days, my desire to live the best life I could and bring value to those I loved was genuine. I could have walked no other path than the one I have trod to get where I am today. Once I realized this, I was finally able to accept myself and be at peace … most of the time.

The Golden Rule

Paralyzed Veterans of America Executive Director Sherman Gillums, Jr., has made it his mission to bring empathy to the Veterans Administration (VA). During an October 2017 C-SPAN Q&A interview he stated, "A lack of empathy … is why the VA found itself in this position where it's now being challenged … ." When asked if it was possible to bring empathy to an organization of some 150 hospitals, 300,000 employees, and a $180 billion budget, he said "That's the $64,000 question." But that is exactly what the Paralyzed Veterans of America is devoted to doing.

Gillums, a former U.S. Marine Corps chief warrant officer, was paralyzed from the waist down in a 2004 auto accident near San Diego, CA. He now conducts trainings for VA administrators and staff, giving them insight into his experience as a patient. He discusses everything from the unaddressed confusion he felt in the hospital right after his injury, to the nightly hospital sounds he endured when trying to sleep, to feeling like a commodity — rather than a human being — when doctors and nurses interacted with him.

We have all heard the Golden Rule: "Do unto others as you would have them do unto you." To know how we would want to be treated in a given situation, we must understand what it is like to be in that situation. This is why empathy is so powerful. VA staff were totally unaware of how their actions came across. When Gillums gave them a "taste" of what it was like to be a patient, they naturally wanted to adjust their behavior and treat their patients as they themselves would want to be treated in similar situations.

When there is no empathy there is no Golden Rule.

I have seen many books and workshops centered on self-sabotage and how to overcome it. What if those sabotage tendencies are parts of ourselves trying to serve us but unaware of their impact, like the VA staffers? What if they are parts of ourselves trying to draw our attention to how we can better minister to the suffering we feel, like Gillums did at the VA? What if we simply don't know ourselves well enough to know what we truly need?

When we are evading or denying who we are, dwelling on the past and its endless cycles of "if only I had..." or focusing on the future and its perpetual scenario generation "what will happen if..." then we become oblivious to the present. We become blind to how we are treating ourselves, blind to how we are treating others, blind to what we truly need, blind to how we can support those we care about.

The Golden Rule and Know Thyself are as inseparable as giving and receiving. You can't have one without the other. When we truly know others, we naturally want to contribute to their well-being. When we truly know ourselves, we naturally want to contribute to our own well-being. From this perspective, talk of self-sabotage holds no resonance.

When we learn how to connect compassionately, both with ourselves and with others, we begin to hear the motivations and love behind our seeming criticisms and destructive behaviors. We begin to make peace with who we are, transforming our relationships with ourselves, family, friends, colleagues, and adversaries. Peace resides at the core of our being. Radiating outward, it heals our world, revealing the loving intentions that surround us.

Born To Care

March 15, 2019: This is not the essay I meant to write this week. Tears cloud my vision as I digest news of the mosque massacres in New Zealand where at least 50 people were gunned down by a member of the white power movement. The grief I feel, the world-wide condemnation, and the countless candlelight vigils testify to the deep love that binds us together. We are born to care. Much of our effort and attention goes to supporting and caring for those we love. We crave connection and feel fulfillment when we know our contributions enhance another's experience.

Words are the most powerful tool we wield. Words describe our world. We use them to classify, organize, and bring coherence to our experience. We use them to dissect events into digestible bits of information that we can comprehend. We use words to forge shared experience, connection, and inclusion.

Words, by their very nature, also cause separation. When we name what something is, we also name what it is not. When the non-profit that I helped found, the Rocky Mountain Compassionate Communication Network, announced its existence in 2010, the question almost immediately arose: Who's included, who's excluded, and how do I fit in? I was caught completely by surprise, stunned that simply naming our group gave rise to the "who's in, who's out" question.

For reasons I cannot explain, in my late teens and early 20s, I studied the rise of Adolf Hitler and the Nazi ideology. I also delved into the Charles Manson murders and the "family" he assembled. When the mass murders in Jonestown, Guyana, occurred I dug beneath the headlines into the details of Jim Jones and his People's Temple. The phenomena leading to mass shootings such as the one in New Zealand are nothing new to me. Words always play a critical role in such events.

Al-Qaeda and Islamic State terrorists call those they kill "infidels." The Nazis called Jews, homosexuals, and Gypsies "sub-humans" and "beasts." In Rwanda, the Hutus referred to the rival Tutsis as "cockroaches." In Australasia, where the New Zealand shooter came from, prominent politicians called Islam "a disease to be vaccinated against." Politicians in the U.S. have referred to people crossing our southern boarder as an "infestation."

Such language arises out of fear and anger, torment and helplessness. It relies on a perception that we are at the mercy of some malignant exterior agency, "my life is a mess because you exist," and that salvation is only possible through eradicating that exterior agency. Using language that creates separation is essential to enabling horrific acts of violence. If we feel any kinship or shared life, it becomes difficult and traumatic to kill.

Fear and anger, torment and helplessness are rooted in disconnection, in the perception that no matter what we do, it will make no difference. They are symptoms of a profound and lonely denial of the self and a resulting isolation from the world. They bespeak a desperate yearning for connection and impact. Using language that promotes connection and inclusion is an antidote to the rampant violence besetting our world. When we experience connection, it is much more difficult for fear to get a hold on our psyche. When we experience connection, we are more present to the impact our presence has.

Empathy is the biggest threat to violent, extreme organizations and movements. It has resulted in members renouncing their KKK affiliation. It was crucial to negotiating the 1998 Good Friday agreement that brought an end to The Troubles in Northern Ireland.

Empathy requires us to be firmly grounded in our own sense of self and secure in our own identity, having the courage of our convictions because we firmly reside within our own truth. Thus, we are not threatened by world views different from our own and can listen to them deeply.

Empathy resides in listening. To empathize, we must become silent and receptive so that the other person's presence registers fully in our awareness. If we are not calm, our own self-talk blocks this receptivity. Hence, empathy begins with listening to ourselves, to our self-talk, creating a self-connection that soothes doubt and weakens the impulse toward internal strife. This inner inclusion and visibility ferments trust. We can then become calm and attentive to others because we have nurtured ourselves. By listening, we shift our own self-talk from a language of separation to one of inclusion, from self-recrimination to self-acceptance; we become more aware that we are, and our presence becomes more vivid. We experience ourselves as co-creators of our own destiny: This is called confidence.

From this confident stance, we can engage others "where they are," for we do not feel threatened. Rather than convince we connect, and they become visible. This visibility invites them into a similarly confident state where they have impact on their own destiny rather than being helpless victims of external forces. This produces a profound shift in perception and becomes a potent act in service of peace and freedom.

When we listen to, rather than hide from, fear and desperation, they reveal themselves as loving devotees to our well-being, simply trying to get our attention and become visible.

At its core, empathy is about visibility, both for the self and for others.

Unconscious By Design

Viktor Frankl, an Austrian psychotherapist and Holocaust survivor, is credited with saying:

"Between a stimulus and a response there is a space. In that space is our power to choose our response. In our response lies our growth and our freedom. The last of human freedoms is to choose one's attitude in any given set of circumstances."

Much of life functions unconsciously. We do not have to tell our heart to beat, our lungs to breathe, or our hair to grow. The ability to move our foot from the accelerator to the brake in a driving emergency or to adjust our balance when we slip — without depending on thoughts to direct the detailed muscular movements — is critical to our safety.

When the amygdala (a part of the brain's limbic system involved in experiencing emotions) senses a threat, it shuts down the thinking brain and shifts priority to muscles and blood flow so our bodies can quickly and energetically respond. This is the stimulus-response mechanism. It's great if you are being chased by a wolf, but the same physical reaction can be stimulated by a potential future event that we hold in our imagination such as what may happen at our next encounter with our ex-partner. Such reactions can also be stimulated by memories like a time you were left alone crying in your room and no one came to comfort you. We may not recognize when present events resonate with past traumas or future fears, so when the stimulus-response reaction sets in we don't always understand why, and we say we are triggered by such and such events. Entire disciplines and industries have grown up around understanding and managing this stimulus-response triggering.

Our stimulus-response mechanisms are unconscious by design. Their purpose is safety and survival in situations where there is no time to think. When imagination triggers stimulus-response patterns at the unconscious level, we often don't understand what is happening; trapped, helpless, or angry feelings may arise. This engenders much misunderstanding, violence, and tragedy.

When we bring this unconscious patterning into conscious awareness, we create the space between stimulus and response that the Frankl quote describes. This enables us to operate out of choice instead of compulsion, which is that "last of human freedoms."

How do we render this unconscious conscious and open that space? The Compassionate Communication answer is observations. Observations are all about noticing what is going on without engaging in criticism, ascribing motive, diagnosing cause, or passing judgment.

We do not discard criticism, motive, diagnosis, and judgment. It is simply that they are likely to trigger unconscious reactions and collapse the space the Frankl quote speaks of, sending us into habitual behavior. Observations, by their very nature, create that space so that we have freedom to choose.

Within the space that observations open:

We can begin to recognize our pull toward compulsive or habitual reactions, bringing the unconscious conscious.

We notice the feelings a situation arouses and feel more fully connected to our being, more fully present.

We listen to the narrative in our minds and can consider how closely it matches our actual experience.

We attune to the sensations in our body and our physiological reactions to the situation.

We consider the information about the environment that our senses — sight, sound, taste, touch, and smell — deliver to our awareness.

All of this enhances our resourcefulness and broadens our perspective so that our actions are more potent and effective. It enables us to, as Henry David Thoreau put it, "learn to live deliberately." We experience life itself as an act of power and our presence as a conscious, creative expression of that power. This awareness instills a stability, an excitement, and a security that words simply can't describe.

Thus, are we free!

Paying Attention

I suspect that all of us have been told at one time or another to "pay attention." A while ago, a friend was confiding in me. She finished speaking, and I realized I had no idea what she had just said. I was so busy thinking, "What she needs to do is ... If only I could get her to understand ... " that I was paying more attention to the story I was telling myself about her than to the flesh-and-blood person in front of me. I was interacting with myself under the guise of interacting with her. The exchange left me with a lonely and dissatisfied feeling, which I then proceeded to blame on her. I sometimes feel deep embarrassment and sadness when I ponder my past self.

While wrestling with this essay, bringing my intention into focus, I spontaneously paused and turned to a computer solitaire game. I made a careless mistake and abandoned the game. "I am not paying attention," I told myself. "My body was going through the motions, but my mind was elsewhere." Suddenly, I realized I had just given myself the focus I was searching for!

When the mind is absent, the body runs on automatic. When the heart is not involved, the mind wanders. Thus, we are not paying attention. When the heart is inspired, the mind focuses, and we become aware of what our bodies are doing. Body, mind, and heart are all engaged, together. We become complete, whole. We become present.

What does it mean to be present? What is it about the current moment that is alive, that nourishes us? What is it that brings body, mind, and heart together?

For me, it is the quality of my relationships, my participation in the world, my connection to life. This is what makes life worth living; how I find joy and fulfillment. When we know that our presence matters, that what we do contributes, and when we feel touched by others, we participate in a shared reality. We are nourished by contributing to a larger whole and are seen for who we are, without pretense.

Yet, our desire to be accepted and safe impels us to hide our perceived inadequacies; we develop a public self, a shield between us and the world. Filtering our experiences and expressions through this public self protects us, but it also separates us from direct experience. Situations where we can drop our public selves become precious, and we treasure those with whom we can be vulnerable.

How do we deliberately cultivate the deep connections that bring meaning to our lives? Is there an authentic core in our depths that can support us while dropping pretense and taking emotional risks?

We all carry parts of ourselves that have been banished to the darkness out of shame, guilt, or fear. When these parts clamor for attention we can look away, denying their existence and precipitating internal strife. Or we can welcome them with tenderness and compassion, allowing these parts to unveil and illuminate the living energy held within. This is the essence of empathy for the self.

Self-empathy leads us to that authentic core in our depths that can feel safe while being vulnerable. Much as a compass guides an explorer through a dense forest, the ability to be aware of our yearnings and to name what is precious provides us with an immensely powerful beacon, drawing us toward fulfillment and joy as we journey ever into the unknown.

Good Grief

One of the most successful of all comic strips was "Peanuts," featuring Charlie Brown. It ran from 1950 to 2000 and was known for the phrase, "Good Grief!"

December 2017: I have been thinking about the phrase "Good Grief!" a lot lately. Grief has been my companion this summer with hurricanes ravaging the Caribbean and Gulf Coast, fires devastating the northwest, hatred and violence on display in Charlottesville, and the insanity in Las Vegas. I shed many tears and trembled with anger. Yet, I resolved to stay anchored in love and compassion and not let recrimination and fear drag me into hatred and despair. Love and compassion demand that I live in authenticity and self-connection, true to my own experiences. Therefore, when recrimination and fear came knocking, rather than send them away I listened deeply and discovered they were but masks for grief. When I could welcome that grief and fully express it, recrimination and fear vanished, and I was left with compassion and resolve.

Thus, grief has been my companion this summer, my authentic response to what I have experienced. Grief has become sacrament, an acknowledgment that I care, a celebration that something is important and touches me. At times it has been intense and uncomfortable, but it has left me rejuvenated, cleansed, vigorous, and feeling more alive, much as a forest is left calm and refreshed with clean air after a robust rain. All in all, I would say, "Yes! Grief is good."

I was recently reading *Foundation and Earth* by Isaac Asimov, published in 1986. As one of the characters in the novel is crying, another one comes up and says, "What's wrong?" This jumped out at me, and I wondered why we assume crying signifies something wrong, something that must be fixed. As I thought about it, I remembered *The Lord of the Rings* by J.R.R. Tolkien, first published in 1954. It contains various scenes of weeping, sometimes with joy, other times in grief, but never portrayed as a malady that must be rectified. It generally indicated that the character was moved deeply by events, responding in a forthright and honorable manner. When, I wondered, did our perspective on tears shift?

I wept when I watched an episode of NOVA about the New Horizons probe that gave us our first detailed glimpse of Pluto, so moved was I by the determination and ingenuity of the NASA team. I wept when Captain Chesley Sullenberger landed his Airbus jet in the Hudson River in January 2009, saving many lives. News reports of Palestinian homes being bulldozed in the West Bank, or Israelis being killed in cafe bombings have also brought tears to my eyes.

I have learned to keep such tears secret because of the discomfort they cause in others. I have been asked "What's wrong?" or "Is everything OK?" or "Is there anything I can do?" I've also been told "Don't worry, everything will be all right." While I was experiencing deep connection with life's preciousness, others perceived suffering. If we are to embrace our humanity and build compassionate culture, shifting our perspective from brokenness and suffering to curiosity and wonder will be instrumental. When we can accept someone as they are and welcome what they are going through with warmth and understanding, this releases stress and dissolves loneliness. It invites us to awaken to what a precious and brief gift life is. Rather than a torment to be endured, life becomes a miracle to be savored.

A dear friend of mine died in a bicycle accident when he was 27. I was 29. The accident happened in California where he had been living for some years. I lived in Denver, as did his family. They went to California and were part of the memorial for his community there. Meanwhile, I became the point person in Denver, attending to the details of setting up a memorial for his Denver community. As the memorial began, I was overcome with grief. I had been holding my feelings at bay as I attended to the logistical details. It felt so good to let go and sob. He was a dear friend and left the world so abruptly. The tears were a celebration, honoring his life.

Suddenly, I felt a hand on mine. A woman I did not know sat next to me. She began patting my hand, saying "There, there." My tears suddenly dried up, and my grief was replaced by anger. I became stiff, my body contracted, and I stared directly ahead. The woman patted my hand one last time, said, "Now isn't that better?" and returned to her seat. I was left with my stony anger, resentful that she had "invaded" my space in a vulnerable moment and deprived me of the bliss I was feeling as I celebrated my late friend's life.

Grief is a part of life. To welcome life is to welcome grief. We grieve because we care. Because we care, we participate. Because we participate, we are connected to life. How can we be truly authentic, fully alive, when we hide from grief and view it as a malady instead of a sacrament?

My Sister

When I first started practicing Nonviolent Communication (NVC), I had the thought, "This means I will have to change my attitude toward my sister. Ughhh, I'm not sure I want to do that."

In conversations with my sister, she often started talking while I was in the middle of a sentence, or she talked so rapidly and for so long that I wouldn't have a chance to speak. When her phone number came up, I'd sigh and think, "Oh man, I guess I have to deal with this." She often came across as angry and domineering. I felt angry in turn and blamed her for "not taking responsibility" and told her to grow up.

Anger was my way of setting boundaries, of protecting myself and not getting too wrapped up in her problems. Yet, I sometimes had trouble going to sleep because I was so busy talking to her in my own head. Still, I was reluctant to give up my protective anger; it did not feel safe to do so. I was afraid of being consumed.

Over time, as my empathy skills deepened, I began to see the world from her point of view. She has severe dyslexia, which makes it difficult to function in a computer-oriented, read-and-write society. Yet, her intellect is strong and her wit sharp. Knowing what she wants to accomplish while finding it difficult or impossible to do so is a frustration she has endured throughout her life.

When she was young, the school system had no idea what to do with her. Her verbal skills were so high that it was not readily apparent that she struggled. She was called lazy or told to simply apply herself. Teachers wondered if she was emotionally disturbed. This had to be hard to take. Being intelligent, she is well aware of the difficulty she encounters where others find ease. I have often heard her refer to herself as stupid. No wonder she can come across as angry.

I began to perceive her as courageous and tenacious, struggling valiantly to exist in a world her brain is not fully equipped to handle. I became amazed at what she has accomplished. Gradually, without realizing it, I stopped blaming her. One day I noticed that my anger had subsided, and my protective barrier had softened. Our connection deepened, her anger diminished, and our conversations became dialogues instead of monologues. I stopped talking to her in my head at night and slept better. Strangely, my boundaries were firmer, and with stronger connection, the dynamic where she tried to cling while I tried to evade dissipated. I began to experience much more autonomy, without struggle, exertion, or forethought. It just happened.

I used to approach our times together with a sense of duty: a necessary family burden. Now I experience pleasure and peace when we interact, for the most part.

This NVC stuff really works!

Still Friends

I was around 20 and house sitting. Having an entire house to myself, I invited a young woman I was very fond of over for dinner. My mind was racing with excitement and expectation about how the evening might unfold. I put on a Judy Collins album and practiced assuming a casual, relaxed demeanor. She arrived, stated she could not stand the music, and left. She was maybe there for 5 minutes. As I heard the front door close, I looked around in a state of shock, totally numb. What just happened, I wondered.

As the evening wore on, I began to feel physically ill. An electrical buzzing began vibrating through my legs, very tense and intense. I tried to relax but could not sit still. Finally, I went for a long walk because my legs were less uncomfortable when I was moving. On returning to the house, I discovered a note stuck to the door. It was from the woman. She stated she did not understand what had happened and why she felt compelled to leave. She went on to state she hated it when we did not get along. A profound relief and ecstasy flowed through my body and especially through my legs. The discomfort immediately left. I went from wondering if I would have to go to the hospital to having a liberating insight into how much feelings affect our bodies.

Our thoughts and feelings have a profound impact on our physiology and vice versa. I have found nothing that describes this relationship more effectively than Compassionate Communication. In the above experience, I was following Compassionate Communication principles, although I was unaware of it at the time.

Rather than raging in my mind and going into blame about the other person or about myself, I became confused, yet curious: What just happened? Consequently, while numb and stunned, I was still calm instead of panicked as the discomfort grew in my legs. When I read the note and felt immense relief flooding my nervous system, I realized how important the relationship was to me. I also became aware of how powerful and influential feelings are. Learning that my date was also distressed reassured me that the relationship mattered to her, that I was not totally off base or delusional about our connection. This provided comfort and let me know she cared just as I did.

To recap in the Compassionate Communication lingo of observations, feelings, needs, and requests:

Observations: I was able to remain calm by observing what was going on and connecting with my body.

Feelings: I listened to my feelings rather than try to distract myself by getting drunk or vegging out on TV, and I got an indelible lesson in how powerfully feelings impact us.

Needs: I realized how much I wanted to matter to another person, how much I wanted to contribute to her life, and how important shared experience is.

Requests: I made a request of myself: Rather than go into rage and blame, I become curious and sought understanding.

Yes, we are still friends to this day.

Spiritual Boot Camp

Often, when we encounter suffering, our spontaneous response is to attempt to alleviate it. Thus, do we express that we care. In personal relationships, one of the ways we try to alleviate suffering is to take on someone else's burden, hoping to relieve them of it, and we get into trying to "fix" them. It becomes easy to lose ourselves, to lose contact with our own authenticity, and to become so wrapped up in the other person's needs that we sublimate or ignore what we need.

We become defined by how they respond to us, and we "wear their story" as if it were our own. "Forgetting" who we are, we lose track of our authentic core. This lack of connection produces doubt, and we are unable to trust ourselves, to trust our own judgment. We become dependent on the other person for direction and meaning. If we want to change our situation, we try to convince them to change so that we can change. This is a formula for confusion and strife where we are ever trying to manipulate the other person in order to feel better ourselves. While we think we are fixing the other person and alleviating their suffering, we are, in fact, perpetuating it. This breeds much argument, desperation, and violence.

Deep within this dynamic is the fact that we care, that there is love struggling to express itself. When we focus on this, we touch something enduring. As we become mindful of this loving intention within us, we naturally begin to see it in the other person also. Blame and recrimination fade as we become aware of the deep needs driving their behavior, and we become less triggered by specific actions. We touch our authentic core and see the authenticity within the other. When we touch that authenticity, stability and security emerge. This feeds our courage, and we dare to trust. Not only do we begin to trust ourselves, we begin to trust the other person. We trust them to meet their own destiny in their own way, and the urge to fix fades. We can then love without condition. Accepting someone the way they are is the most empowering and loving act we have to offer. We literally place confidence in them, which invites them to have confidence in themselves.

For me, this is not abstract. I raised my nephew from the time he was 3 until he was 19, when schizophrenia emerged. After several intense visits to emergency rooms, he was placed in a psychiatric hospital where he remained for many months.

This was the most difficult circumstance I have ever metabolized. I had to come to terms with the fact that no matter how much I loved my nephew, no matter how much I wanted things to be different, I could not fix his dendrite-depleted brain. I came to the conclusion that the most I could do for him was to love him and trust him with his own destiny. For someone whose life had revolved around rescuing, this was immensely difficult.

I could not help but reflect on what my nephew's future held. I would often dwell on moments from our past. Such musings were tearing me apart. I started calling it "spiritual boot camp." I said it was like having a stick up my you-know-what, impelling me to transform or die. Could I "walk the talk" and follow the prescriptions I had been giving others, based in my many explorations into human consciousness? Those prescriptions centered around trust, authenticity, empathy, and being present to and welcoming what is.

At one point I recalled a time when my nephew was 3. I was lying on my back. He ran at my foot. I grabbed his arms, and with my foot on his chest, rolled back onto my shoulders, launching him through the air and onto the pillow-filled couch. His body filled with laughter and his face aglow with excitement, he gained his footing, rushed back to my feet, and we did it again. And again. And again. And again…

In the midst of that reverie, as I felt again the joy of that moment, a most amazing insight surfaced: My nephew's current condition did not in any way detract from the beauty and fulfillment of that fun on our couch. I realized that all the times I spent with him and all the sacrifices that I made were precious because they were precious, not because they were payment due on some past account, nor because they were an investment in some future pay-off.

In that instant, I realized that every moment is complete. Seed, flower, blossom, root, and soil, it is the source of its own fulfillment. It owes nothing to the past; it owes nothing to the future. Owing nothing, the present moment is free, unbounded, without compulsion. The impulse to hide and submit subsides. Likewise, the desire to control and dominate vanishes.

Life is lived in present tense; even when we remember the past or ponder the future, we do so now. When I am in the present moment, story drops and words do not define or confine me. I know without a doubt that I am, and it is enough.

I started this book describing my journey to a mountain top. I end with an essay recounting the closest I have come to regaining the extraordinary state of consciousness that I experienced on that mountain top.

And thus we build a bridge between us
And learn to climb above aloneness
Into a land of companionship secure
That can withstand the darkest loneliness
And evaporate it into fearless playful glee
When on a relentless commitment to freedom we agree
That we need only be who we are and nothing more:
To explore what's implicit in such a commitment
Is what this entire book, this entire lifetime, is for.

A Note About
Observations, Feelings, Needs, And Requests

The genius of Marshall Rosenberg's work lay in his system for metabolizing experience by viewing it through the prism of observations, feelings, needs, and requests. This structure is referenced in several places in the book. I add this brief explanation to provide clarity for the reader who is not familiar with Rosenberg's work.

> **Observations:** When we train ourselves to observe what is going on as objectively and clearly as possible, this creates a space for us to act deliberately.

> **Feelings:** We then listen attentively to our feelings, which brings us fully present and expresses our connection to what is happening.

> **Needs:** Listening to feelings, we become curious about the deep underlying values or needs that matter to us and motivate our behavior.

> **Requests:** Finally, we consider what actions are most likely to honor or fulfill our needs, and we make requests. We use requests to emphasize working in "power with" others, rather than trying to dominate or having to submit.

Consequently, we decrease the likelihood of violence.

These steps lead to a profound empathy that awakens compassion, dissolves the illusions that separate us, and draws us into our common humanity, which is only possible because we are connected so deeply to our own values that our identity and boundaries are secure. Thus, we build community by honoring autonomy.

Authenticity Meditation

This meditation is designed to promote understanding and restore balance when something upsets or troubles us. It helps dissolve stereotypes and penetrate labels, revealing the heart-felt motivations that propel our actions as well as the actions of others. This enables us to stay connected to authentic essence and create connections that sprout security and peace.

I suggest you have someone read the meditation to you or record it yourself and play it back. It can also be found at the livelovenow.life website, read by me.

Pick the situation you want to work with. Pick something where there is discomfort coupled with a yearning for deeper connection, or more understanding, or peace and calm. It can be a direct encounter with someone, or something you saw from a distance, or something you read or heard.

Invite your reaction to the situation to be present now. It may help to write down what happened and how you responded.

When you are ready, get comfortable and close your eyes. Take a moment to check in with your body and ask it if there is anything you can do to make it more comfortable.

Part 1: Connecting With What You Care Deeply About

Step 1. Notice your present state, how this recollection lives in your body now. Your thoughts may start racing, parts of your body may clench, you may notice that your thoughts are so active that you lose track of what is going on around you — other people speaking, for example. You may experience an uncomfortable tingling, a heaviness in your stomach, or feel a cold brittleness.

Step 2. Pause and take a breath. Feel the breath move down into your chest. Follow it as it leaves your body and another breath enters. Continue this for several breaths.

Step 3. Listen to what your thoughts say. Notice the pitch, cadence, and volume of your thoughts. Take a moment, just listen, observe what happens. Perhaps there are images or sensations that accompany your thoughts. Maybe feelings arise. Simply notice what is happening.

Step 4. Check in with your body. Are there any tensions or constrictions? Do the tensions or constrictions shift as you notice them? Are they trying to communicate something to you? Be still and listen.

Step 5. Repeat Steps 1 through 4 until you feel expansion or comfort in your chest or softening in your muscles. Your breathing may naturally move to the foreground of your awareness while your thinking moves to the background.

Step 6. Now, ask yourself: How does being upset support me? What am I protecting? What yearnings or values are so precious that my body has mobilized all of this energy to serve them?

Step 7. Put your attention on what you are protecting, on what is precious. Notice any memories this may bring up. Observe the pitch, cadence, and volume of your thoughts. Do feelings emerge? What are the sensations in your body? What is your breathing doing?

Step 8. Why is this preciousness so important to you? Why do you care about it? What does it want for you? What actions provide a living example of this preciousness?

Step 9. Call to mind the situation that was originally upsetting to you. Notice any differences in the way you now perceive it.

Step 10. If your body is constricted or tense, you can go back to Step 2. If you are feeling complete for now, this would be a good place to stop. If you want to delve further into understanding the situation, continue to Part 2.

Part 2: Connecting With The Other

Step 11. Recollect what was originally upsetting to you. Ask yourself, why would someone behave the way they did or believe what they expressed? Why are they so energized? What may they hold precious? What are they protecting?

Step 12. Put your attention on what you guess the other is trying to protect, on what you believe they may hold precious. Notice the pitch, cadence, and volume of your thoughts. What are the sensations in your body? Do feelings emerge? What is your breathing doing? If you are feeling too constricted to continue, you can stop at this point or you can go back to Step 2 and repeat the process.

Step 13.   Invite into your body the preciousness or motivation that you guess the other values. Doing so, do you feel threat? Is there understanding? Just observe. You do not have to "do anything" about your experience. Simply notice how you react.

Step 14. If you have an understanding of their possible core motivation, how would you express that in a way that is congruent with your own values? Give it a try.

Step 15.   Reconnect with what you yourself hold precious. Is there a way you could express your own core values that the other might understand, that they are unlikely to perceive as a threat or challenge?

Step 16. Considering any insights into the other's core motivations and what you yourself hold dear, is there overlap? How do they differ? Is there another value you hold that embraces both of them?

Step 17. Is there a concrete action or expression that authentically honors both values? Maybe the answer is no, maybe it is yes. Simply observe. Check in and see if you can hold the other person in your awareness without feeling threatened. Bring your attention back to your breathing, your body, your thoughts, your feelings. Observe what is alive in your awareness at this moment.

Step 18. Take 5 minutes to go into stillness and silence, anchored in your breathing. When you are ready, gently open your eyes and return to the room.

Journaling, dancing, gardening, or walking in nature are all excellent activities to follow this meditation and allow it to settle and integrate.

About The Author

Poet, writer, and life coach, David Steele has studied and taught a wide variety of interpersonal communication skills over the last 30 years. Co-founder of the Rocky Mountain Compassionate Communication Network, David aspires to freedom, both personal and communal, and has an unwavering devotion to the well-being of the planet.